THE ARRAS WITCH TREATISES

MAGIC *in* HISTORY

SOURCEBOOKS SERIES

The Magic in History Sourcebooks series features compilations and translations of key primary texts that illuminate specific aspects of the history of magic and the occult from within. Each title is tightly focused, but the scope of the series is chronologically and geographically broad, ranging from ancient to modern and with a global reach. Selections are in readable and reliable English, annotated where necessary, with brief contextualizing introductions.

SERIES EDITORS

RICHARD KIECKHEFER,
Northwestern University

CLAIRE FANGER,
Rice University

THE ARRAS WITCH TREATISES

Johannes Tinctor's
Invectives contre la secte de vauderie
and the
Recollectio casus, status et
condicionis Valdensium ydolatrarum
by the Anonymous of Arras (1460)

Edited and translated by
ANDREW COLIN GOW,
ROBERT B. DESJARDINS,
AND FRANÇOIS V. PAGEAU

The Pennsylvania State University Press
University Park, Pennsylvania

Library of Congress
Cataloging-in-Publication Data

Names: Gow, Andrew Colin, editor,
translator. | Desjardins, Robert B.
(Robert Byron), 1969– , editor,
translator. | Pageau, François V.,
1963– , editor, translator. |
Tinctor, Johann, approximately
1405–1469. Sermo contra sectam
Valdensium. English. |
Anonymous of Arras. Recollectio
casus, status et condicionis
Valdensium ydolatrarum. English.
Title: The Arras witch treatises :
Johannes Tinctor's invectives
contre la secte de vauderie and
the Recollectio casus, status
et condicionis Valdensium
ydolatrarum by the Anonymous
of Arras (1460) / edited and
translated by Andrew Colin Gow,
Robert B. Desjardins, and
François V. Pageau.
Description: University Park,
Pennsylvania : The Pennsylvania
State University Press, [2016] |
Series: The magic in history
sourcebooks series | Includes
bibliographical references and
index.
Identifiers: LCCN 2016002011 |
ISBN 9780271071282 (pbk. : alk.
paper)
Subjects: LCSH: Witchcraft—
France—Arras—Early works to
1800. | Demonology—France—
Arras—Early works to 1800.
Classification: LCC BF1582 .A155
2016 | DDC 133.4/30944272—dc23
LC record available at http://lccn.loc
.gov/2016002011

CONTENTS

ACKNOWLEDGMENTS

The project of editing and translating into English the rich and extensive collection of documents pertaining to the Vauderie d'Arras began in 2005, with the discovery of a manuscript copy of Johannes Tinctor's *Invectives contre la secte de vauderie* in the Bruce Peel Special Collections at the University of Alberta. Then director Janine Green and librarian Jeff Papineau offered us extensive support and advice as we set out to analyze the codex and translate the remarkable treatise it contains. Since Janine's retirement, we have been fortunate to have the assistance of Linda Quirk, the assistant director. Together with director Robert Desmarais, Linda and Jeff have supported our work in countless ways.

A number of other people have been instrumental in bringing this project to its present state. Pat Dutchak and Rhonda Kronyk both did many hours of careful work on the text of the *Invectives,* making a number of important discoveries about the provenance of the Alberta manuscript. Erik Kwakkel of Leiden University expertly analyzed the codex, and Paula Simons, a feature writer with the *Edmonton Journal,* undertook independent research to help us understand how it arrived in our city. (Her subsequent coverage informed Canadians about the significance of the treatise, and of the Vauderie d'Arras more generally, as did the fine documentary produced by Dave Redel of CBC Radio's *Ideas.*) James White patiently read through our translation of the *Invectives,* noting a number of potential problems and errors. Jessica Roussanov offered helpful comments on our introduction, and Suzanne Wolk copyedited the final manuscript perceptively and with great care.

We would also like to acknowledge the many contributions made by students in Andrew Gow's demonology seminar in the fall terms of 2013 and 2014. Matthew Punyi, Rita Neyer, Elisabeth Hill, and Jeffrey S. Longard in particular stimulated our thinking; Jeffrey's extensive and thoughtful glosses on the *Invectives,* and on the scriptural and patristic references contained in the treatise, helped to improve and expand our explanatory references. We are grateful for all of these contributions.

Finally, we wish to thank the series editors and the many people at the Pennsylvania State University Press who have contributed to our project. It is thanks to their interest and enthusiasm that this volume is now in readers' hands.

MAP 1 The Duchy of Burgundy around 1460. The black lines show modern borders.

Introduction

The Arras Witch Treatises in Context

On a spring day in 1460, in the bustling city of Arras,[1] in northern France, a crowd of merchants, artisans, and farmworkers gathered to witness a grim spectacle. A scaffold had been erected in the local bishop's courtyard; on it stood a Dominican inquisitor and five defendants accused of spectacular crimes against the church. The prisoners—four prostitutes and an eccentric poet—were dressed in the robes of public penitents. Each wore a miter on which an image of the accused worshipping the devil had been painted.[2] Nearby on the stage lay the corpse of another prisoner, a sergeant named Jean Lefebvre, who had died in jail under suspicious circumstances.[3]

Gesturing at the group, the inquisitor, one Pierre Le Broussard, denounced them in a loud voice. These vile women and men, he said, had been involved in *vauderie*—diabolical witchcraft. He rattled off a list of their crimes:

When they wished to go to [worship the Devil], they anointed a small stick of wood, and their palms and their hands, with

1. The events described here took place in the *cité* (as opposed to the *ville*) of Arras. Medieval Arras comprised two sectors: the *cité*, which was under the jurisdiction of the bishop, and the town, which was administered by a council of aldermen. The bishop enjoyed both temporal and spiritual power in his bishopric.

2. Miters were used as instruments of public shaming in heresy, sorcery, and witchcraft trials.

3. According to Jacques du Clercq, "the night before their sentence was rendered, he was found hanged and suffocated in prison by the end of his hood, and the truth of whether he hanged himself or was hanged, for fear that he would accuse others, will never be known." (All translations are our own unless otherwise noted.) See Jacques du Clercq, *Mémoires de Jacques du Clercq sur le règne de Philippe le Bon, duc de Bourgogne*, 2nd ed., vol. 3, ed. Frédéric de Reiffenberg (Brussels: Lacrosse, 1836), 4.4.20 (the numbers refer to book, chapter, and page).

an ointment that the Devil had given them. Then they put the branch between their legs, and soon they were flying themselves . . . to the place where they were to have their assembly . . . and there they found the Devil in the form of a goat, of a dog, of an ape, and sometimes of a man.

And they . . . paid homage to the Devil, and adored him, and most of them gave him their souls. . . . [T]hen they kissed the Devil in the form of a goat on his posterior, that is, on the anus, with candles burning in their hands. . . . And after paying this homage, they trod upon the cross and spat upon it, in defiance of Jesus Christ and the Holy Trinity; and then they showed their anus toward the sky and the heavens, in defiance of God.[4]

According to Jacques du Clercq, a local chronicler who recorded the spectacle, Le Broussard went on to accuse the defendants of feasting and fornicating with the devil; of pulverizing consecrated hosts so as to blend them, together with the bones of toads and the blood of children, in foul magical ointments; and of committing other foul deeds.[5]

The terrified suspects all confessed to the charges—confessions they later recanted, protesting that they had been promised clemency in exchange for a guilty plea. They received no such mercy; all five were burned at the stake.[6] This appalling event was one of the first in a series of episodes that would explode into a full-blown witch hunt. By the time it was over, thirty-one people had been convicted, many on the basis of confessions extracted through torture. Thirteen had been burned at the stake. The city's business had been disrupted, its commercial networks damaged, and its reputation deeply tarnished.

---

4. Ibid., 4.4.21.

5. We suspect that Du Clerq worked from the original trial records (which were later burned), largely because he used specific legal language and formulations that were characteristic of such records, and were quite distinct from his style elsewhere.

6. A fifth prostitute, one Belotte Moucharde, was fortunate to escape execution that day. As Du Clercq reports, this was thanks to the fact that "her miter had not been finished." She remained in prison until October 1460, when she was expelled from the diocese and sentenced to go on pilgrimage (ibid., 4.15.75–76). See below.

Yet this was not just a local tragedy. The Arras affair, known to French scholars as the Vauderie d'Arras, is in fact a highly significant event in the history of witch-hunting. It was one of the earliest and most prominent cases in which "state" prosecutors in an urban setting used the so-called elaborated theory of witchcraft as a basis for interrogating, torturing, and executing large numbers of people.[7] The story that Pierre Le Broussard told in the courtyard of the bishop of Arras—with its themes of night flight, secret meetings, devil worship, fornication, desecration of hosts, preparation of ointments, and infanticide—was markedly similar in content and tone to accusations that would be launched time and again in ecclesiastical and secular courts across the continent over the next 250 years, leading to the execution of tens of thousands of women and men.[8]

BACKGROUND: ARRAS AND ITS INQUISITORS

Like many of the large-scale witch hunts that followed it, the Arras affair had its theological roots less in the town square than in the meetings and conversations of learned churchmen—notably Dominicans. Traditional accounts, based on the testimony of Du Clercq, hold that the Vauderie d'Arras was precipitated in the fall of 1459 by the trial of an unusual man, a Franciscan hermit named Robinet de Vaux, at a meeting of Dominicans in Langres.[9] Like the Arras defendants, de Vaux was charged with *vauderie*—a deceptive term with a complex

7. The "elaborated theory" (or "cumulative concept") of witchcraft was a composite narrative combining a number of accusations traditionally leveled at groups of feared and despised "others." See below.

8. Though exact numbers will never be known, it has been estimated that some sixty thousand people were executed across Europe during the witch trials of the sixteenth and seventeenth centuries. At least half of these executions took place in the German-speaking lands of the Holy Roman Empire.

9. The Dominicans were mendicant friars and preachers committed to bringing dissidents back to the faith through public disputation—and, when that failed, by serving as members of inquisitorial courts. They had provided the intellectual fuel for inquisitorial practice since the thirteenth century. On this subject, see Christine Caldwell Ames, *Righteous Persecution: Inquisition, Dominicans, and Christianity in the Middle Ages* (Philadelphia: University of Pennsylvania Press, 2009).

etymology. Originally referring to "Waldensianism," a religious movement persecuted by church authorities in the preceding centuries, the
word had undergone a semantic shift.[10] In the minds and writings of
inquisitors and theologians, it had come in some cases to signify a
particularly monstrous form of diabolism and witchcraft.[11]

De Vaux implicated at least two other people in his alleged crimes
before being convicted and executed. Both of the accused lived in the
region around Arras, in the northern territories of the duke of Burgundy, an independent-minded vassal of the French king. Unfortu-
nately for the two—a prostitute named Deniselle Grenier and a
traveling poet-performer named Jean Lavite—one of the Dominicans
present at the proceedings in Langres was Pierre Le Broussard. He
was the inquisitor of Arras and, as Du Clercq notes, he took action
after he returned home. Both the *femme de folle vie* and the poet, a
member of a troupe of performers who had been nicknamed "the
Abbot of Folly," were arrested and brought to the city.[12]

Interrogated and tortured, the pair began to name names, accusing many of their contemporaries of participating in *vauderies*, a term
used in the plural to refer to witches' conventicles, or "Sabbaths." Their
accusations produced a wave of paranoia in the town, residents of all

10. On the history of the Waldensians, see Gabriel Audisio, *The Waldensian Dissent: Persecution and Survival,
c. 1170–c. 1570*, translated by Claire
Davison (Cambridge: Cambridge University Press, 1999).

11. This was in fact a complex (and
far from linear) evolution. A 1440 letter from Pope Eugenius IV is one of
the first official sources to use
"Waldensian" as equivalent to "witch."
On the relationship between heresy
and diabolical witchcraft and the evolution of the term *vaudois*, see Hans
Peter Broedel, "Fifteenth-Century
Witch Beliefs," in *The Oxford Handbook of Witchcraft in Early Modern
Europe and Colonial America*, ed.
Brian P. Levack (Oxford: Oxford University Press, 2013), 32–49; Richard
Kieckhefer, "The First Wave of Trials

for Diabolical Witchcraft," in ibid.,
159–78 (esp. 166–68).

12. Stuart Clark argues that there
is a symbolic link between the activities
of witches and those of the protago-
nists in popular festivals. The fact that
the "Abbot of Folly" was accused of
playing the role of "Master of Ceremo-
nies" at a Sabbath (see below) rein-
forced his "inverted" festival identity.
See Clark, *Thinking with Demons: The
Idea of Witchcraft in Early Modern
Europe* (Oxford: Oxford University
Press, 1999). For a useful study of the
confréries joyeuses, of which the
"Abbot" was a member, see Katell
Lavéant, "Théâtre et culture dramatique d'expression française dans les
villes des Pays-Bas méridionaux
(XVe–XVIe siècles)" (PhD diss., University of Amsterdam, 2007).

classes fearing that they might be named next. These anxieties were soon borne out, as a group of vicars, urged on by Le Broussard and other senior churchmen, conducted an ever-widening investigation.[13] The circle of the accused grew to include servants, sergeants, wealthy burghers and aldermen, and even, near the end of the craze, a lesser nobleman named Colard de Beaufort. The city itself, meanwhile, became increasingly isolated from its neighbors. Travelers from Arras had trouble finding lodging in nearby towns; their hosts, says Du Clercq, were fearful of being drawn into the web of accusations.

The trial described above, in which both Deniselle and the "Abbot of Folly" were denounced and executed, was one of several such scenes to play themselves out over the course of the summer and autumn of 1460. Because of the frequent and brutal use of torture, each new group of arrests produced a new wave of accusations. In this pattern of violent coercion, fear, and inflationary prosecution, as in the nature of its accusations, the Vauderie d'Arras anticipated the much larger witch crazes of the sixteenth century. Indeed, far from being a result of medieval superstition and cultural decline, the Arras affair was the harbinger of a new and aggressive mode of persecution on a continent that, for all its supposedly "modern" developments, would become far more "superstitious," far more steeped in diabolism and demonology, in the decades and centuries that followed. A great deal about this kind of persecution was entirely new, owing as much to new modes of thinking—"scientific," religious, and magical—as to medieval ideas.[14]

But unlike many later panics, the Arras campaign spent its force relatively quickly. The inquisitors had overreached by trying and convicting such prominent figures as the nobleman Beaufort. He and some of his co-accused appealed the case to the Parlement de Paris, or royal law court. Duke Philip of Burgundy put a stop to the arrests

---

13. The leading players in the Arras affair included Le Broussard; Jacques du Bois, the dean of the cathedral chapter of Arras; and the suffragan (or assistant) to the absent bishop of Arras, one Jean Fauconnier (who was also the titular bishop of Beirut). The vicars, led by Pierre du Hamel, included Jean Pochon, Jean Thibaut, and Mathieu du Hamel.

14. See Anne Lawrence-Mathers and Carolina Escobar-Vargas, *Magic and Medieval Society* (London: Routledge, 2014) on this topic as well.

in Arras, and the inquisitors quickly found themselves on the defensive, their campaign discredited. One of the most tenacious prosecutors, Jacques du Bois, suffered a mental breakdown; the bishop of Arras, who had been absent during the affair, returned home and took his deputies to task for overstepping their authority. Beginning in early 1461, the Paris appeals shined a light on the warped logic and vicious excesses of the prosecution. The Parlement eventually ruled in favor of the defendants, ordering their complete rehabilitation and pardon, and the return of their confiscated property—though for a variety of political reasons, the court's *arrêt*, or judgment, was not completely enforced until 1491.[15]

Yet short-lived as the Vauderie d'Arras turned out to be, the events in this northern French town are of singular importance to those seeking to understand and analyze the European witch hunts. This is because in addition to being one of the earliest mass prosecutions based on the elaborated theory,[16] the Vauderie d'Arras played itself out in a highly developed urban society that had no shortage of writers—chroniclers, lawyers, and intellectuals—to take note of events. Few fifteenth-century trials have bequeathed us so many texts, so much raw and candid description, in part because many other trials left little or no record beyond a brief notice in a record of court decisions. And of all of these texts, the most important from the perspective of intellectual history are a pair of treatises—one written by a respected scholar from a nearby town, the other penned by one of the Arras inquisitors—on the nature and dangers of this "new sect" of witches.

These two texts, which we present in this volume, made a unique contribution to a decades-old debate that had already produced a small body of scholarly treatises and shorter essays on diabolical witchcraft. In addition to engaging with some of the most important

15. On the complexities of this process, which was deeply influenced by changing political circumstances, see Franck Mercier, *La Vauderie d'Arras: Une chasse aux sorcières à l'Automne du Moyen Âge* (Rennes: Presses Universitaires de Rennes, 2006), 13 and passim.

16. There is, to be sure, evidence that witch hunts of a similar size had occurred somewhat earlier, most notably in regions around the modern Swiss and French Alps. See Richard Kieckhefer, *European Witch Trials: Their Foundations in Popular and Learned Culture, 1300–1500* (London: Routledge, 2011), 106–47 (esp. 124–33).

controversies of the time, they brought with them the insight and authority of men who had seen and participated in events that other intellectuals had only interpreted from a distance. Our authors were part of the inquisitorial machine that sent Deniselle, the "Abbot of Folly," and many others to their doom. To understand how this experience empowered them to contribute to the "witchy" ideas that were circulating among fifteenth-century intellectuals, we must look briefly at the evolution of demonological ideas, and in particular the elaborated theory of witchcraft, in the years leading up to the Arras affair.[17]

THE ROOTS OF THE ELABORATED THEORY

What, then, was this "elaborated theory"? What it was not is a monolithic or coherent set of principles that some sociopathic churchman had dreamed up in a fit of paranoia or repressed rage. Le Broussard's accusations reflected a composite stereotype—a bundle of ideas drawn from various medieval sources and traditions—that had gradually come together in the minds of scholars and inquisitors in the decades preceding the Arras trials. One of these ideas, the notion of promiscuous secret meetings involving orgies, cannibalism, and infanticide, was nearly as old as Christianity itself; it was first leveled against Christians by Roman pagans in the second century C.E.,[18] and in the intervening period it was turned against groups regarded as dangerous to the faith—among them members of "heretical" sects such as the Cathars.[19]

---

17. We use the term "elaborated theory" with care, mindful of the risks of reducing a complex, evolving, and multifaceted set of beliefs to a simplified ahistorical concept. For a nuanced discussion of the regional alternatives to and variations on the "classic paradigm of diabolical witchcraft," see Kieckhefer, "First Wave of Trials"; and Richard Kieckhefer, "Mythologies of Witchcraft in the Fifteenth Century," *Magic, Ritual, and Witchcraft* 1 (Summer 2006): 79–108.

18. See Norman Cohn, *Europe's Inner Demons: The Demonization of Christians in Medieval Christendom*, rev. ed. (Chicago: University of Chicago Press, 1993), 1–15.

19. See Jeffrey Burton Russell, *Witchcraft in the Middle Ages* (Ithaca: Cornell University Press, 1984), 88–95, 120–32, 219–25; Brian P. Levack, *The Witch-Hunt in Early Modern Europe* (New York: Pearson Longman, 2006), 40–45; Cohn, *Europe's Inner Demons*, 35–78.

Other elements of the theory were of more recent vintage. While accusations of devil worship had also been leveled at heretical groups for centuries, they were exacerbated here by an anxiety, rooted in the fourteenth century, over elite ritual magic involving compacts with Satan.[20] In stark contrast, tales that witches used magic to harm their neighbors' property, and that they flew through the night sky on shafts of wood, were probably rooted in common notions about folk magic.[21] Beginning in the late fourteenth century, all of these ideas came together in stages to form a kind of noxious ideological stew—as the catalysts of real-life witchcraft trials, especially in the Alps,[22] and as a basis for learned treatises.

The impetus for the latter occurred around the time of the Council of Basel (1431–49), when church thinkers began trying to rationalize the strange reports of devil-worshipping witches and protracted trials reaching them from sites such as Simmental (ca. 1395–1405) and the Valais (1428). Johannes Nider's *Formicarius* (*The Anthill*), penned in the mid-1430s, presents a "partial, uncertain and contradictory" effort to come to terms with these new ideas about witchcraft.[23] Treatises written in the same period by the Swiss judge Claude Tholosan and an anonymous cleric of the Val d'Aosta region likewise contained key elements of the emerging theory.[24]

20. See Cohn, *Europe's Inner Demons*, 102–43; Levack, *Witch-Hunt*, 37–40; Alain Boureau, *Satan the Heretic: The Birth of Demonology in the Medieval West* (Chicago: University of Chicago Press, 2006), 69–92.

21. See Cohn, *Europe's Inner Demons*, 162–80, 211–33; Levack, *Witch-Hunt*, 45–50; Russell, *Witchcraft in the Middle Ages*, 75–82.

22. See Kieckhefer, *European Witch Trials*, 10–26 (esp. 18–26), 106–47.

23. Carlo Ginzburg, *Ecstasies: Deciphering the Witches' Sabbath* (Chicago: University of Chicago Press, 2004), 70. An excerpt from the *Formicarius* translated into modern French, appears in Martine Ostorero, Agostino Paravicini Bagliani, and Kathrin Utz Tremp, eds., *L'imaginaire du sabbat:*

Edition critique des textes les plus anciens (1430 c.–1440 c.) (Lausanne: Université de Lausanne, 1999), 120–99; for an overview of the text, see Martine Ostorero, *Le diable au sabbat: Littérature démonologique et sorcellerie (1440–1460)* (Florence: SISMEL, Edizioni del Galluzzo, 2011), 29–33. See also Michael D. Bailey and Edward Peters, "A Sabbat of Demonologists: Basel, 1431–1440," *Historian* 65, no. 6 (2003): 1381–85.

24. Editions (and modern French translations) of Tholosan's treatise, and of the *Errores Gazariorum*, are presented in Ostorero, Bagliani, and Tremp, *Imaginaire du Sabbat;* for an overview of both texts, see Ostorero, *Diable au sabbat*, 33–41. See also Ginzburg, *Ecstasies,* 73; Bailey and Peters, "Sabbat of Demonologists," 1388–91.

The authors of these early tracts, and of a host of essays that followed them, agreed on a number of the constitutive features of diabolical witchcraft. A few questions, however, caused ongoing controversy. Did the devil really enable witches to fly through the air to secret gatherings? Was this in keeping with the doctrine articulated in the canon *Episcopi*, an important article of tenth-century ecclesiastical law proclaiming such phenomena to be mere illusions caused by the devil? One of the most strident statements supporting the reality of night flight came the year before the Vauderie d'Arras, when the Dominican inquisitor Nicolas Jacquier penned his *Flagellum haereticorum fascinariorum*. The treatise affirmed, among other things, that witches do indeed fly through the air; and given that their sect practiced a new kind of heresy, inquisitors need not concern themselves with the spirit or implications of the canon *Episcopi*.[25]

Like Jacquier, the authors of our treatises—Jacques du Bois, dean of the cathedral chapter at Arras,[26] and Johannes Tinctor, canon of Tournai—spent part of their careers in French Flanders; like him, they were trained in Scholastic method.[27] But it is a testament to the fluid state of ideas about the witches' Sabbath that our two authors didn't necessarily agree with Jacquier, or with each other, about certain of these ideas, which were debatable on the grounds of both contemporary and traditional perspectives. Some notions, such as claims about night flight, collided with inconvenient precedents in theology and canon law (not to mention practical human experience). Others, such as the need to understand whether demons could impersonate innocent people during Sabbaths, or how recantations on the deathbed (or more accurately, at the stake) were to be dealt with, spoke directly to the problems involved in prosecuting large groups of people for fantastical crimes in accordance with accepted legal practice. Together, they point to the richness and complexity—and fundamental instability—of the ideas expressed in our two treatises. A few notes about

25. Bailey and Peters, "Sabbat of Demonologists," 1393. On Jacquier, see Matthew Champion, "Scourging the Temple of God: Towards an Understanding of Nicolas Jacquier's *Flagellum haereticorum fascinariorum* (1458)," *Parergon* 28, no. 1 (2011): 1–24.

26. We do not know for certain that Du Bois was the author of the *Recollectio*, but scholars believe he is the most probable candidate; see below.

27. Tinctor and Jacquier even lived in the same city, Tournai, at points in the 1460s—the former as a canon, the latter as an inquisitor.

the two intellectuals and their work will help to position and contextualize these ideas.

THE AUTHORS AND THEIR TEXTS

It is important to observe, first of all, that while Du Bois and Tinctor were very different sorts of men, occupying different stations in medieval Burgundian society, a few key attributes united them. One of these is the intellectual tradition of Scholasticism: a product, like the Inquisition, of the confident and expansive intellectual culture of the twelfth and thirteenth centuries. In simple terms, Scholasticism approaches theological questions with a focus on Aristotelian rationalism and systematic argumentation.

This means that a modern reader approaching a Scholastic text for insights into the worldview of its authors must be prepared to encounter content that is unfamiliar, even opaque. By the fifteenth century, Scholastics traded in a very specialized language; they drew from a wide body of claims and conceptual formulas, many of them centuries old. Yet modern readers untrained in the nuances of the field can still benefit from reading Scholastic treatises critically. They can be attentive, for example, to aspects of emphasis: to the types of questions asked by a text, the types of authorities to which it appeals, and the ways in which its appeals are made. They can examine rhetorical strategies and omissions: the use of contents derived from sources, the omission or adaptation of contextual arguments present in those sources, and the neglect of sources that might contradict the author's thesis. Finally, and most fundamentally, they can contextualize this analysis by considering what Gabrielle Spiegel has called the "social logic" of the text: the ways in which it speaks to the social, cultural, and political milieu that informed it.[28] With this in mind, it is useful to inquire into the historical conditions

---

28. See Spiegel, "History, Historicism, and the Social Logic of the Text," in Spiegel, *The Past as Text: The Theory* *and Practice of Medieval Historiography* (Baltimore: Johns Hopkins University Press, 1997), 3–28.

surrounding these texts, and the lives of the men who (probably) wrote them.

Jacques du Bois and the Recollectio

The *Recollectio casus, status et condicionis Valdensium ydolatrarum* (*A History of the Case, State, and Condition of the Waldensian Heretics [Witches]*) was written in the spring or summer of 1460, shortly after the first groups of alleged *vaudois* had been tried in Arras. While the author is not identified in either of the surviving copies of the treatise—an early version held at the Bibliothèque royale in Brussels, and a later version contained in a bundle of contemporary writings on demonology housed at the Bibliothèque nationale in Paris[29]—the text reveals that he was present at the first trial, on May 9. This evidence, together with other textual and biographical features, has convinced several scholars that the fanatical Jacques du Bois was probably the elusive Anonyme d'Arras responsible for this chilling work.[30]

Regrettably, little is known about Du Bois himself. The dean of the local cathedral chapter, he was about thirty-five years old at the time of the Arras trials—an ambitious young man, as the scholar Franck Mercier remarks, whose star was on the rise.[31] It was he, writes chronicler Jacques du Clercq, "who took the greatest pains in interrogating Deniselle,"[32] the first of the accused, and he who secured the help of the powerful Count of Estampes to spur on the local vicars when their enthusiasm for the hunt was waning. He also seems to have aroused more resentment among townsfolk than nearly any other figure in the affair.[33] Summoned by the Parlement de Paris in early

29. Brussels, Bibliothèque royale, MS 11449–51, fols. 1r–33r; Paris, BnF, MS lat. 3446, fols. 36r–58r.

30. See Mercier, *Vauderie d'Arras*, 32; Ostorero, *Diable au sabbat*, 666; Émile van Balberghe, "Les oeuvres du théologien Jean Tinctor," in *Les manuscrits médiévaux de l'abbaye de Parc: Recueil d'articles* (Brussels: Ferraton, 1992), 130 (esp. n. 2); Dyan Elliott, *The Bride of Christ Goes to Hell: Meta-phor and Embodiment in the Lives of Pious Women, 200–1500* (Philadelphia: University of Pennsylvania Press, 2012), 271.

31. Mercier, *Vauderie d'Arras*, 32.

32. Du Clercq, *Mémoires*, 4.3.11.

33. An anonymous satirical verse distributed in Arras in the fall of 1460, taking to task all of the key prosecutors in the affair, addressed Du Bois first. Ibid., 4.16.82.

1461 to answer the appellants, the dean "succumbed to a delirious illness and seemed to take leave of his senses"; and while some in the city "felt pity" for him, writes Du Clercq, "there were also many who said that this was God's punishment." Though he recovered his faculties, Du Bois never regained his health. He died in early 1462 after suffering "terrible torment" from bedsores.[34]

THE *RECOLLECTIO*: STRUCTURE AND RHETORIC

Reluctant as we may be to project psychological categories into the past, it is hard not to observe that the mental breakdown described in Du Clercq's text is remarkably consistent with the sorts of paranoid fantasies and sublimated desires expressed in the *Recollectio*.[35] Of its various contributions to the emerging theory of witchcraft, the treatise is perhaps most striking for its detailed, obsessive, and often visceral depictions of the Sabbath. The first four of the essay's thirteen articles deal with the particulars of the witches' nocturnal sins, from their temptation by demons and allied human agents, to their flight to the Sabbath, and, finally, to their formal admission into the diabolical sect.[36] Several elements of the elaborated theory are blended together here: from night flight (article 2), to the diabolical pledge and the Black Mass (article 3), to the desecration of hosts and infanticide (article 4).

The social landscape of the late medieval Low Countries casts a long (and often recognizable) shadow over these passages, which seem especially haunted by threats to ecclesiastical authority from groups of feared or despised "others." Some of these groups, the "usual suspects," are easy to anticipate. Following the lead of earlier essayists on diabolical witchcraft, for instance, the Anonymous presents a telling analogy between Jews and the *vaudois*. The Sabbath, in his parlance, is a "synagogue" (articles 3 and 4), and the

34. Ibid., 4.26.128–29.

35. In suggesting this, we do not mean to exaggerate the likelihood that Du Bois's incapacity, illness, and death resulted primarily from psychological factors; it is entirely possible that the underlying problems were physical in origin.

36. See Mercier, *Vauderie d'Arras*, 71–75.

leaders of the sect are its "rabbis" (article 11).[37] Prostitutes, and women in general, are likewise targeted, their role in the Sabbath carefully emphasized and delineated (article 3).

Alterity, however, is not the only source of anxiety in the *Recollectio*. As Franck Mercier has observed, the devil presiding over the Sabbath clearly prefers, and places emphasis on, influential and well-placed minions (see articles 3, 6–8). This may suggest that the fears that inform the text relate not primarily to the threat of social revolution but rather to that of institutional corruption.[38] The author, that is, may fear that Christendom is about to be infiltrated by apocalyptic evil—or that the infiltration has been under way for some time.[39]

The story of the witches' Sabbath, then, is a tale concerned with many things other than witches. Throughout his text, moreover, the author is both catholic (in the traditional sense) and practical in his approach, setting out to grapple with the thorny (and often paradoxical) legal problems involved in prosecuting people accused of *vauderie,* a relatively novel crime. Articles 6 through 11 are primarily concerned with questions of jurisprudence and procedure that had confronted the prosecutors in the first Arras trial.[40] They seem to have been crafted both to reinforce the choices made during that trial and to anticipate any criticism they might provoke, whether they involve the use of torture in witchcraft proceedings (article 6), the validity of witches' accusations of others (article 7), or the inadmissibility of recantations of confessions (articles 9 and 11).

Accordingly, these passages provide vivid snapshots of the plight of the accused in Arras. In article 8, the Anonymous writes that witches' accusations against their accomplices should not be dismissed simply because *nonnulli dicunt* (some people say) that demonic impersonation is possible. "Some people," we may assume,

---

37. For a useful discussion of these terms, see ibid., 71. It is worth noting that while the term "synagogues" is used frequently in the context of the witches' Sabbath, the Anonymous's use of "rabbis" to refer to leaders of the *vaudois* is more unusual, and extends the anti-Judaic and apocalyptic logic of this semantic field.

38. Ibid., 73.

39. This is one concern that the Anonymous appears to share with Tinctor; see below.

40. See Mercier, *Vauderie d'Arras,* 32–33.

had raised this very objection either at or in connection with one of
the early trials in Arras. This is one of many references to the events
of the Vauderie d'Arras sprinkled throughout this text—references
that carry real historical value. In addition to reinforcing our conviction that the author probably was Du Bois, the "prime mover" of the
prosecutions, they enable us to triangulate with other records so as
to gain a clearer sense of what happened at the trials.[41] They make
explicit reference to many of the accused—from the "Abbot of Folly,"
to Belotte ("Cutie") Moucharde, a prostitute, to Jeanne d'Auvergne, the
madam of a local brothel—and they offer us an indirect but palpable
sense of the motives, methods, and approaches of the prosecutors.

A NOTE ON OUR TRANSLATION OF THE *RECOLLECTIO*
While P. G. Maxwell-Stuart has provided a fairly complete translation
of the *Recollectio* in his recent collection of primary sources in translation ("The Waldensians, Their Sabbat, Their Evil Deeds, and How
to Prosecute Them, Anonymous, 1460," in *Witch Beliefs and Witch
Trials in the Middle Ages: Documents and Readings* [London: Contin-
uum, 2011], 79–114), we feel that the passages that he left out—notably
the opening section, which draws on Scholastic theology and on
Aquinas in particular to state a case for the reality of spiritual creatures and the possibility that their actions can have real effects in the
physical world—are critical for understanding the project as well as
the intellectual background and significance of this treatise in historical context. There were also too many places where we disagreed with
Maxwell-Stuart's translation of the quite thorny late Scholastic Latin,
and so we decided to publish our own complete translation of this
strange text. We remain deeply indebted to Maxwell-Stuart for working out a number of passages that we had previously been unable to

---

41. The trial records, as noted
above, were burned as part of the decision of the Parlement de Paris following the appeals launched by Colard de
Beaufort and others. Thus we have only
indirect testimony to these events, in
the form of such texts as Du Clercq's
Mémoires and the records of the
appeals. There is a high degree of cor-
relation between the methods of interrogation recommended in the
Recollectio and those reported in the
appeal records as having happened at
Arras.

decipher, and for his erudite comments. We have tried to acknowledge our use of his work whenever appropriate.

Johannes Tinctor and the *Invectives*

Who was Johannes Tinctor? It is best to begin by acknowledging who he was not. Our temptation to classify such men as Du Bois using modern psychological categories ("fanatical," "mentally unstable," and the like) can mislead us when we consider the careers of other medieval demonologists and witch-hunters. So it is with Tinctor. Far from being a bloodthirsty sociopath or attention-seeking eccentric, the author of the *Invectives* was a respected intellectual who had written widely about more benign subjects. We have no reason to doubt that he was motivated by, among other things, a desire to enlighten his readers about a threat he regarded as truly dire, and stakes he believed to be world-historical.

Beyond that insight, however, our understanding of the life and thought of this curious man is limited by the range of available sources, which include his scholarly and hortatory works and a few historical references. We know that he was born around 1405 in Tournai, a city whose bishop (like that of Arras) played an important role in contemporary politics. We also know that he was a successful scholar at the University of Cologne, rising through the ranks to become dean of arts in 1433, dean of theology (then regarded as the university discipline with the greatest prestige and seniority) in 1442, and, by the middle of the century, rector of the university.[42]

Throughout his career, Tinctor was "fairly prolific," as Jan Veenstra notes in his study of the *Invectives*. His work included commentaries

---

42. See Jan R. Veenstra, *"Les fons d'aulcuns secrets de la théologie:* Jean Tinctor's *Contre la Vauderie;* Historical Facts and Literary Reflections of the *Vauderie d'Arras,"* in *Literatur-Geschichte-Literaturgeschichte,* ed. Nine Miedema and Rudolf Suntrup (Frankfurt am Main: Peter Lang, 2003), 436; Bernard Bousmanne, Frédérique Johan, and Céline van Hoorebeeck, eds., *La librairie des ducs de Bourgogne: Manuscrits conservés à la Bibliothèque royale de Belgique,* vol. 2, *Textes didactiques* (Brussels: Bibliothèque Royale de Belgique, 2003), 258.

on Aristotle, on Aquinas, and on Peter Lombard's *Sentences*—all key sources of study for Scholastics. He also produced "a number of theological treatises (on the Eucharist, on miracles, and the like) and a number of sermons and official speeches and addresses."[43] His work continued after his appointment as a canon in Tournai, the city in which he retired in 1460 and died in 1469. As a corpus, it was—if not towering—certainly respectable in the eyes of his contemporaries.[44]

Tinctor himself was active in the witch craze. "During his final years in Tournai," as Veenstra notes, he "apparently became involved in the persecution of the vaudois." He "played a part in the arrest of three or four people on the charge of vauderie" and turned his pen to the challenge of avenging their injuries to Christendom.[45] He wrote at least one public sermon scolding a man for devil worship; and, most significantly, he wrote the *Invectives* in Latin and translated it (or had it translated) into Middle French.[46]

THE *INVECTIVES*: STRUCTURE AND RHETORIC

Tinctor appears to have been motivated by a variety of concerns when he crafted the *Invectives*. The first, and most pressing, was no doubt the need to justify the prosecutions that were taking place (or had recently taken place) in Arras. But his text makes no direct mention of these events, and it becomes clear early in the treatise that Tinctor also had higher theological and political objectives in mind. One of these was to call on earthly authorities to make war against a sect of people guilty of deeds so evil that they might serve as a catalyst for the apocalypse. Another was to contribute to a scholarly debate around elements of the "elaborated theory," such as the idea of night flight by diabolical means, that strained credulity—and that thinkers in previous centuries might have regarded as laughable.

---

43. Veenstra, *"Fons d'aulcuns secrets,"* 436.

44. On Tinctor's writing and thinking, see also Frédéric Duval, "Jean Tinctor, auteur et traducteur des *Invectives contre la secte de Vauderie*," *Romania* 117, nos. 1–2 (1999): 186–217;

Van Balberghe, "Oeuvres du théologien Jean Tinctor," 123–53.

45. Veenstra, *"Fons d'aulcuns secrets,"* 436.

46. On Tinctor's goals for the French translation, see Duval, "Jean Tinctor."

In pursuing these goals, Tinctor crafted a three-part treatise that is strikingly uneven in both tone and content. The prologue, which provides a cosmological framework for the discussion of witches, is far less evocative than the first major section, which harangues prelates and princes to do away with the sect. That part is, in turn, far less "scientific" than the second major section, which purports to answer a range of technical questions about the "witches" and their practices—and, in so doing, joins up with several of the demonological debates we have already outlined.

The most notable of these questions is one to which both Jacquier and the Anonymous devoted considerable intellectual energy: the reality of physical transportation by the efforts of the devil. For his part, Tinctor is clearly uneasy about contradicting the canon *Episcopi*, and is careful to qualify his claims about the reality of night flight and other diabolical "miracles" against nature. He hedges on the critical point of the reality of such miracles: whether witches were actually transported through the air by demons to their nocturnal orgies or only imagined that they had been, they were equally guilty in either case because they willingly participated. Actually sinning and merely intending to sin come down to the same thing in Christian doctrine, he argues. This is a hinge on which many witchcraft prosecutions in the following centuries would turn: was it enough to actually cause harm by diabolical means, or was merely wanting to, or attempting to, sufficient for conviction? Tinctor understands the objection and moves decisively to block it using this clever maneuver.

Over the course of his treatise, Tinctor deploys his full range of professional weapons—rhetoric, logic, and Scholastic learning—in an effort to alarm, to provoke, to educate, and even to reassure his readers. His book takes an important place in the growing corpus of scholarly texts that predated, prefigured, and prepared the groundwork for the publication of the infamous *Malleus Maleficarum*. And indeed, of the two foul witch treatises of Arras, Johannes Tinctor's book—with its more conventional, more nuanced ideas, which constitute a more authoritative discourse—is by far the fouler and more dangerous one. It is the text with the greatest power to influence people and events.

Not surprisingly, therefore, Tinctor's book enjoyed a wider distribution. Not only did it circulate among churchmen in Latin, but it reached the Burgundian and French (and probably also the English) courts in lavish, illustrated Middle French manuscript copies (ca. 1465) that are still extant.[47] It was one of the first books to be printed in French in the Low Countries—by Colard Mansion, sometime after 1475.[48] While it was not much cited in later years, the ideas and fantasies it advocated were echoed in the better-known *Malleus*, printed in 1487—a best seller by comparison.[49]

We cannot, of course, establish a direct genealogy that shows how either Tinctor's treatise or that of the Anonymous influenced or contributed to the *Malleus*, or to any other text. But we can observe that ideas about diabolical witchcraft seemed to be circulating among a group of relatively prominent intellectuals in the second half of the fifteenth century. Tinctor and the Anonymous (Du Bois) made their own contributions to that circulation around 1460, and the author of the *Malleus* would be able to draw on them in the 1480s, across the Rhine and a few hundred miles upriver. Precisely how those ideas were communicated we do not know, but they were the same ideas, circulating among members of the same group of intellectual specialists, and with chillingly similar effects.

A NOTE ON OUR TRANSLATION OF THE *INVECTIVES*

We offer this translation, the first into English, in the hope that it will help expand and enrich the debate about the genesis and timing of the "elaborated theory" of diabolical witchcraft, not merely among specialists who can read the original texts but also among students and lay readers. Our translation grew out of our reedition of the text based on a previously unknown manuscript (one of four now known) that we discovered by chance, miscatalogued and unrecognized, in the University of Alberta Library (Bruce Peel Special Collections).

---

47. Paris, BnF, MS fr. 961; Brussels, Bibliothèque royale, MS 11209; Oxford, Bodleian Library, MS Rawlinson D 410.

48. Jean Tinctor, *Invectives contre la secte de vauderie* (Bruges: Colard Mansion, n.d. [between 1476 and 1484]).

49. See Christopher S. Mackay, *The Hammer of Witches: A Complete Translation of the Malleus Maleficarum* (Cambridge: Cambridge University Press, 2009)."

A History of the Case, State, and Condition of the Waldensian Heretics (Witches) (1460)

ANONYMOUS OF ARRAS

In his collection of late medieval texts and treatises related to witchcraft, Joseph Hansen introduces this text as follows:[1]

> The manuscript of this tractate is found in Ms. Lat. 3446 at the Bibliothèque nationale. . . . The manuscript, however, is not an original but a copy, as one can see from the many errors in writing and copying. The following printed version is based on this manuscript. . . .
>
> The treatise was written in Arras immediately after the first trial against the [witches] was brought to a close in May of 1460, probably during the preparations for the second trial, which the treatise was designed to facilitate by explaining the actions taken during the first trial. The unknown author was . . . personally present at this trial, and heard the confessions of the accused himself.[2] He describes himself as *minus in sacris eloquiis et philosophorum sentenciis doctus* (someone not especially learned in sacred eloquence and in the teachings of the philosophers), and is therefore trying to

1. Hansen, *Quellen und Untersuchungen zur Geschichte des Hexenwahns und der Hexenverfolgung im Mittelalter* (Hildesheim: Georg Olms, 1963 [first publ. 1901]), 149 (translated from the German). Our translation of the Latin *Recollectio* (*History*) is likewise based on the transcription that appears in Hansen's *Quellen und Untersuchungen*, 149–83. As Hansen notes here, he derived his text from BnF, MS lat. 3446 (fols. 36r–58r), one

of two known manuscript copies of the *Recollectio*; we have also consulted this manuscript. (A second copy of the treatise is held in the Bibliothèque royale in Brussels: MS 11449–51, fols. 1r–33r.)

2. A number of references in the text create this impression; some of these appear in the introduction (p. 20) and in articles 1 (pp. 27–30), 7 (pp. 54-57), 8 (pp. 60, 63), and 12 (pp. 72–75).

produce the impression that he was not one of the inquisitors involved in the trial. The treatise, which was written with the express purpose of justifying the trial as conducted by the inquisitors, and which offers reasons for further trials, stems, as he admits, from inquisitorial circles.[3]

We have used brackets to indicate subheadings that we inserted to help readers navigate through parts of the text. These subheadings do not appear in the original manuscripts.

A HISTORY OF THE CASE, STATE, AND CONDITION OF THE WALDENSIAN HERETICS,[4] written from the notes and treatises of many inquisitors and other experts, and principally from the confessions and trial records of those same witches at Arras, in the year of the Lord one thousand four hundred and sixty.

Zeal and fervor for the Catholic faith, which should burn in any faithful Christian, compels this writer to depict in writing a history of the case, state, and condition of the witches from the notes and treatises of many inquisitors and other experts, and from the confessions and trial records of those same witches, wherein those things which illuminate reason and knowledge are submitted for polishing and correction by anyone of better knowledge. Those things, however, which depend upon experience and practical knowledge will be reported faithfully for all men.

And indeed, if the public were to think that some of those things originated merely in the opinions of this writer, who is not especially learned in sacred eloquence and in the principles of the philosophers, and who lacks experience of many things, they would not be inclined to give them any more credence than they would to the ideas of every-

---

3. Hansen, *Quellen und Untersuchungen,* 149. Hansen goes on to speculate that Pierre Le Broussard, the inquisitor of Arras, was the author or source of the *History.* Scholars have since argued convincingly that Jacques du Bois, the dean of the cathedral of Arras, was the more likely author (see introduction, p. 11).

4. "Waldensian heretics," "Waldensians" (hereafter "witches").

one else. For there are as many meanings and opinions as there are minds, and as Horace says, there are a thousand types of men, but no single desire rules all lives.[5] Therefore, this treatise will be organized in sections, on which more in the following.

1. ON THE POSSIBILITY AND, INDEED, THE REALITY OF THE ACTUAL CORPOREAL TRANSPORTATION OF WITCHES BY DEMONS TO THEIR CONGREGATIONS

It is well known to anyone who is learned in philosophy and sacred letters that demons can transport the bodies of human beings from place to place, especially when they consent to it and when God permits it, because of the sins of those same people and of their heresy. Why, therefore, could not any demon, by virtue of his creation, be able to do this with no other faculty attributed to him after his creation? However, the power of demons is restricted by the divine will, lest it break out against men; for it is restricted by the blessed angels, and it is limited and diminished by the mystery of our redemption and by the passion of Christ our Savior. For from his side flowed the sacraments of the church; armed with them, human beings are able to resist these demons. In the order of created beings, the purely spiritual creatures, that is to say, the good and evil angels, stand out by virtue of their superior natural gifts. Indeed, the evil angels or demons retained their natural gifts even after they sinned.

And Lucifer himself, now the Prince of Darkness, when he was created, was the highest ranking of spiritual and intellectual creatures. And for that reason, the Devil, both by virtue of the way he was created and because of his own power, is able to transfer and transport through

5. This quotation is actually taken from Persius, *Satire V* 52–53: "Mille hominum species, et rerum discolor usus / Velle suum cuique est, nec voto vivitur uno" ("There are a thousand human types and their experience varies; / Each have their own wishes, and no one desire rules every life," trans. A. S. Kline). Persius (Aulus Persius Flaccus, 34–62 C.E.), an Etruscan satirist with Stoic inclinations, was deeply influenced by Horace (65–8 B.C.E), one of the most prominent lyric poets of the Augustan era. For Kline's translation of the *Satires*, see http://www.poetryintranslation.com/PITBR/Latin/PersiusSatires.htm. For the original Latin version, see https://archive.org/details/satirarumliber cuoopersuoft.

space so great a thing as a town, with everything inside it, to some other place, no matter how vast the distance; or to put one town in the place of another, without tiring in any way, because he never tires. [He can do this] either because God has relaxed his vigilance, or has granted his express permission, without the addition of any new power from any source whatsoever. Therefore, the Devil is all the more likely to be able, suddenly, and so quickly that we cannot perceive it, to transport a man from one place to another, just as far as he wants, with the knowledge and permission of God the just, on account of that man's infidelity and his sins. On this, the doctors [of the church] are united.

And this possibility is inductively and indirectly supported by the article of the [Apostles'] creed *creatorem coeli et terrae* [creator of heaven and earth]. So far as this article is concerned, the created order leads back ultimately to God. Indeed, God created all things in a certain and proper order, in which the good and evil angels, because they are spiritual creatures, deserve the first and highest rank. And since they are spiritual, and contain no matter in their composition, nor can they be reduced to any definite matter, they can transport from place to place, as they like, any material or physical things, whether from side to side or up and down, if God permits. The holy doctor addresses this quite broadly in the first part of his *Summa*,[6] going well beyond the works of the other holy and illustrious doctors. Even the master of the *Sentences*, Peter Lombard, covers it, especially in the seventh section of book 2,[7] as does Scotus

---

6. As Hansen notes, this passage refers to Thomas Aquinas, writing in his *Summa Theologiae*. Just as Augustine of Hippo (354–430 C.E.) had contributed enormously to early medieval conceptions of the devil, Aquinas (1225–1274), the most prominent of all Scholastic thinkers, helped to shape the evolution of later medieval demonology. His reflections on the nature and capacities of angelic beings were particularly influential in this regard (see, e.g., *ST* I, Qs. 51–53 and 110–14). For a useful discussion, see Fabián Alejandro Campagne, "Demonology at a Crossroads: The Visions of Ermine de Reims and the Image of the Devil on the Eve of the Great European Witch-Hunt," *Church History* 80 (September 2011): 479–87.

7. Peter Lombard (ca. 1096–1160) wrote *Four Books of Sentences*, a collection of biblical, patristic, and scholarly sources that became one of most influential theological texts of the Middle Ages. Book 2 is titled "On the Creation and Formation of Things Corporal and Spiritual" (trans. Alexis Bugnolo); a number of chapters in its seventh section (or "distinction") consider effective power of demons in the material world. For information on Bugnolo's translation of the *Sentences*, see http://www.franciscan-archive.org/lombardus/II-Sent.html.

in the second of his writings,[8] and Bonaventure addresses it even more broadly.[9]

However, for the great author Dionysius[10] (according to whom the divine wisdom joined the ends of the first things to the foundations of the second), it is necessary that the lower nature, according to its subordination, be joined to the superior nature.[11] And for this reason, it is necessary that corporeal nature (in which local movement is prior and more perfect compared to other kinds [of movement], since it does not decay, nor is it converted into anything of substance, as Aristotle teaches) can be moved locally by angelic nature, which is incorporeal and secondary. And it follows that an angel, whether good or bad, can, by affecting corporeal nature alone as well as the other types, cause beings and objects to move through the application of any kind of local motion. However, no one should doubt that a certain great power of the corporeal elements of this world was brought together by the Creator. This power is latent in various sparse seeds of corporeal nature. When they are brought into relationship with one another in various ways, there are miraculous results. And all these things can be obtained through angelic action, according to the truth of the created order.

8. John Duns Scotus (ca. 1266–1308), a prominent Scholastic thinker, produced a sophisticated commentary on Lombard's *Sentences*. This is the work, as Hansen notes (151), to which this passage refers.

9. Bonaventure (Giovanni di Fidanza, 1221–1274) was, like Aquinas and Scotus, an influential (and highly prolific) Scholastic philosopher. As Hansen notes (151), the Anonymous seems to be referring here to Bonaventure's commentary on book 2, distinction VII of the *Sentences*.

10. Dionysius the Areopagite, a fifth- or sixth-century writer known today as Pseudo-Dionysius, wrote philosophical texts with Neoplatonist and mystical attributes. He wrote pseudonymously, attributing his work to a man said to have been converted by Paul in the Acts of the Apostles (17:34). His writings dealt, among

other things, with the celestial hierarchy and the relationships between various levels of being. For more on Pseudo-Dionysius, see Rosemary A. Arthur, *Pseudo-Dionysius as Polemicist: The Development and Purpose of the Angelic Hierarchy in Sixth Century Syria* (Aldershot, UK: Ashgate, 2008).

11. The argument that follows, beginning with this citation from Dionysius, appears to be assembled from several passages in Aquinas's *Summa Theologiae*, including I, Q. 110, Arts. 3 and 4, and I, Q. 18, Art. 1. Tinctor provides virtually the same sequence of citations in the *Invectives*, though in a slightly expanded form (see below, p. 127–28). Possible explanations for this concordance include the use of a common source, consultation between the two authors, and one author copying another's ordering.

To prove this possibility one can adduce the following: the pact by which the Devil (Matt. 4) placed Christ on the roof of the temple; the account of Simon Magus, who was lifted up by the Devil and flew through the air, as Saint Leo, pope and *pontifex maximus,* recalls in the *Legenda aurea* on the life of Saint Peter the Apostle; and the account concerning Saint Anthidius [*sic*], archbishop [*sic*] of Bithynia.[12] For whatever any man, by whatever possible knowledge, industry, science, or human art, can do in a human way regarding the limits of local movement in however long a time, the Devil can do all these things—not instantaneously, for there can be no local movement in an instant, but in an extremely short time. This movement may be so incredibly quick that it is imperceptible to us. [The Devil may] open or close the damper of a fire, reveal any kind of hidden thing, separate and rejoin objects, etc., in the blink of an eye, as will appear in the following. For man moves those same things in the external world using tools; God, however, worked without tools and without any preexisting material when he created [the universe]; and angels and the Devil [work] with preexisting material and with tools.

And indeed,[13] as regards the reality and truth of the transportation of wide-awake human beings in body and soul to these meetings, which the witches practice, this appears from the confessions and trials of those witches themselves. For this reality is substantiated and confirmed, as the preceding small treatise[14] shows in the section *Sanctam ecclesiam catholicam.* For indeed, the church punishes the idolatrous witches in many regions, not on account of dreams or fantasies or illusions—for in a dream or while dreaming we do nothing of merit or demerit[15]—but on account of their real transportation and movement by demonic means. [They are brought] to their con-

---

12. Probably refers to Saint Anthimus of Rome (d. 303), reportedly born in Bithynia. Anthimus is said to have been saved by an angel after being cast into the Tiber River with a stone tied around his neck.

13. As Hansen notes (151), the following inscription appears in the margin of BnF, MS lat. 3446, in which this version of the *Recollectio* appears: "Incepe-

runt Valdenses heretici anno domini MCLXX" (The Waldensian heretics originated in the year of the Lord 1170).

14. "This treatise is not in the manuscript [BnF, MS lat. 3446] and cannot be found." Ibid.

15. Here the Anonymous takes a position markedly different from that of Tinctor. See "A notice to judges" in the *Invectives,* below (p. 138–39).

gregations on those occasions by their own consent, and on account of the most evil deeds they commit, there or elsewhere, by the order and command of the Devil.

Saint Augustine, in his book *De doctrina christiana*,[16] seems to deal appropriately in a few places with the possibility [or] reality of the actual transportation of the idolatrous witches of whom we are now speaking.[17] And in fact, Vincent [of Beauvais], in his *Speculum historiale*, drawing on Hélinand of Froidmont [*Chronicon*],[18] presents the example of a gathering of Waldensians[19] around three hundred

16. Augustine of Hippo (354–430 C.E.), the early church father who was most revered (and most influential) in the medieval West, wrote widely on the subject of demonology. For a useful discussion, see Campagne, "Demonology at a Crossroads," 475–79. *De doctrina christiana* (397–426 C.E.) is a guide, in four books, to reading, understanding, and teaching the scriptures.

17. As P. G. Maxwell-Stuart notes in his translation of this text (contained in *Witch Beliefs and Witch Trials in the Middle Ages*, 80), Augustine deals with the pacts between humans and demons (referring to 1 Cor. 10:20: "I do not want you to become associates of demons"), but not with the transportation of humans by demons.

18. Vincent of Beauvais (ca. 1190–ca. 1264) was a Dominican intellectual who wrote and compiled the *Speculum maius* (*Great Mirror*), a sprawling encyclopedia of medieval knowledge. The *Speculum historiale* (*Historical Mirror*), the most widely read and distributed part of the encyclopedia, offered an overview of human history. As the Anonymous suggests, Vincent based his history on the *Chronicon*, a vast global chronicle compiled between 1211 and 1223 by Hélinand of Froidmont (ca. 1160–ca. 1230), a Cistercian writer and poet.

19. This is the first in a series of references in which the Anonymous seems first to draw parallels between historical Waldensianism and the contemporary (imaginary) crime of diabolical witchcraft, and then to distinguish the two concepts. Historical Waldensianism (named after its founder, Valdès) emerged in Lyon in the second half of the twelfth century. Waldensians promoted ideas, such as voluntary poverty and lay preaching, that church authorities soon came to regard as subversive. Adherents were declared heretics in 1184 (and again in 1215), and were persecuted harshly beginning in the early thirteenth century. Over time, Waldensians were accused of incest, promiscuity, and devil worship (see Cohn, *Europe's Inner Demons*, 51–61). By the mid-fifteenth century, the term *vaudois* had taken on a broader usage, and referred to (presumed) practitioners of diabolical witchcraft, even when those individuals had no connection to Waldensianism per se. Here, in suggesting that a group of historical ("real") Waldensians gathered in a forest, the Anonymous seems to be drawing parallels between their method of traveling and communing and that of the contemporary "witches." The reference to Vincent of Beauvais, however, is apocryphal; there is no such passage in the *Speculum historiale*, as both Hansen and Maxwell-Stuart note.

years ago in a certain forest close to Arras, where the bishop of Rheims and the provost of Aire are mentioned. Moreover, in the second part of the book *De donis spiritus sancti,* in the fifth chapter,[20] on the powers of Christ's holy cross that cause demons to flee, we find the case of a certain priest who provides a complete description of this damnable sect of idolatrous Waldensians;[21] and in the *Golden Legend* there is a mention in the life of Saint Basil of some girl handed over for marriage, etc., where the faith of the Waldensians is clear enough to see.[22]

However,[23] the heretical Waldensians, or the Poor of Lyon, and Albigensians, who reigned around 270 years, more or less, were dif-

20. Hansen provides the following context for this reference: "This concerns the book *De septem donis spiritus sancti* [On the Seven Gifts of the Holy Spirit] by the Dominican and inquisitor Étienne de Bourbon, active around 1250 (edited under the title *Anecdotes historiques, légendes et apologues tirés du recueil inédit d'Étienne de Bourbon,* published by A. Lecoy de la Marche in Paris in 1857)" (152). Étienne (Stephen) of Bourbon (d. ca. 1261) was a Dominican inquisitor and writer whose *Seven Gifts,* an instructional text for preachers, referred to some contemporary heretical beliefs. As Maxwell-Stuart notes, the passage in question, which appears in a section of the *Gifts* devoted to the "gift of force," provides an overview of the origins of the Waldensians (*Anecdotes historiques,* 290–93). For a useful study of the text, see Pekka Tolonen, "Medieval Memories of the Origins of the Waldensian Movement," in *History and Religion: Narrating a Religious Past,* edited by Bernd-Christian Otto, Susanne Rau, and Jörg Rüpke (Berlin: De Gruyter, 2015), 165–88, esp. 174–77.

21. Meaning real Waldensians, as above.

22. Hansen says, "This concerns only the story, found also in Jacobus

de Voragine's *Golden Legend,* of a pact with the Devil, which St. Basilius (d. 379) dissolved. The citation of this story with the addition '*ubi professio Valdensium satis declaratur*' [where the faith of the Waldensians is clear enough to see] is especially characteristic of the author of this treatise" (152). Jacobus de Voragine (ca. 1230–1298) was a Dominican theologian and archbishop of Genoa; his *Golden Legend* contained a collection of saints' lives and other inspirational texts. The story in question, as Maxwell-Stuart notes (80n74), involves a slave who, having made a pact with demons to win the love of a wealthy man's daughter, repents of his actions. This reference reiterates the long-standing claim that (historical) Waldensians were guilty of demonic invocation; it is a charge that continued to play an important role in beliefs about contemporary "witches."

23. Hansen notes, "In the margin: 'Pauperes de Lugduno, Valdenses heretici et Albigenses, qui regnabant tempore Ludovici, patris sancti Ludovici regis Francie'" (152) (The poor of Lyon, heretical Valdenses and Albigensians, who were at their height during the time of Louis, father of Saint Louis, king of France).

ferent [from today's witches]. They belonged to a very different sect; for they were open heretics, as we see in the book *De donis,* but the witches are not, properly speaking, heretics, but worse, for they are secret and occult idolaters, apostates, infidels, blasphemers, etc. And the judges note that female or male soothsayers, and those who invoke demons, if they are questioned correctly, mainly turn out to be witches, and are of that sect. For all witches [nowadays], by virtue of their essential and formal profession of faith, or their acceptance into their congregation, consider themselves on that account to be invokers of demons—even if not all such invokers are witches—but demon invoking and witchcraft often coincide.

[The reality of the crime, the role of inquisitors, and the forms of punishment]

First, we must note in advance and in general that as regards the witches, there are three points. The first point regards the possibility that this damned sect truly travels to their meetings, and that this sect [actually does] the other things [that they are said to do]—that is to say, whether both human sexes are transported through space to their damnable congregations in body and soul, alive and awake, while exercising all of the functions of human creatures. If people deny that this is possible, it can be shown to be true and real by recourse to learned men, especially those thoroughly instructed in sacred letters. For now in Arras, the real existence of these is appearing, clear as day, thanks to those men whose job it is to investigate this matter, and to other serious and learned men of good zeal and upright judgment.

[Yet] there is no need on this first point to have recourse to learned men or theologians. For certain evidence should be enough to demonstrate the reality of these matters happening without any deception of the senses, namely, the confession of those witches who were really and truly, while alive and awake, transported in body and soul to this or that place by the Devil, and who do not claim to have been asleep, because they were transported through space to this or that place—because if someone were dreaming that he was in another place, he would not say that he had been in that place; rather, he would say that he had been dreaming it, and that he had not really been there. Nor do the canon *Episcopi* and the chapter *Nec mirum,*[24] etc., [contradict this], since they are two different things and not opposed to each other, as one can clearly see by looking and considering both cases. For the Devil sees he is not worshipped and adored openly and manifestly in images or by other means in Christianity, as was the case at the time of the heathens, because punishments are now inflicted on those who openly worship him; [therefore he] transports those same "Christians" at night, with God's just permission, to most secret places, in order to be adored and venerated clandestinely.

The second point in this matter is the investigation of an individual and the legal process to determine whether or not he is a member of this sect. And for this task, theologians, and a few honest, faithful men of great zeal who are especially well versed in this matter, are necessary, for a few experienced men can succeed much better in these tasks than any number of learned men who have no experience of them. For this matter is highly unusual, and for that reason the means of proceeding, and everything related to them, cannot be based on other cases. [This is true,] first, because in the particular case of the witches much is hidden, below the surface, and secret. We normally have no way of discovering this crime except by [the witches'] own confession or by that of accomplices who, in such cases, can be and must be the only accusers and witnesses. Neither reputation, nor good company, nor pretended outward signs of devotion, nor any other such things, which must be weighed in other cases—and which can increase or decrease, or even remove, suspicion—have any large role to play here. And second, [this is so] because the Devil has great

24. This refers to a passage in the *Decretum Gratiani;* Hansen notes (153) that the text in question is causa 26, quaestio 5, canon 14 (see also Maxwell-Stuart, 81n76). The *Decretum,* compiled by the twelfth-century jurist known only as Gratian, is a volume of canon law that was in effect in the Roman Catholic Church until the early twentieth century. The passage in question played a key role in promoting and licensing the skepticism regarding the reality of witchcraft (and particularly of night flight) that was previously articulated in the tenth-century canon *Episcopi.* Indeed, the relevant text from the *Episcopi* was itself reproduced in Gratian's volume (causa 26, quaestio 5, canon 12). For a useful overview, see Alan Charles Kors and Edward Peters, eds., *Witchcraft in Europe, 400–1700: A Documentary History,* 2nd ed. (Philadelphia: University of Pennsylvania Press, 2001), 72–77.

power over witches, since they are practically deserted by God, and because the Devil, by his malice, subtlety, and power, offers them his full assistance (with the just permission of God, whom they forsake entirely). The Devil himself suggests and implants responses or impedes them lest they accuse themselves or others, as will be seen in greater detail below.

The third point is determining the appropriate level of punishment—major or minor—depending on the severity and number of their crimes. As concerns any particular case, the number of accomplices must be weighed, as well as how important it is to deter the people from such crimes through public punishment—and in brief, all circumstances that require attention. Learned men with particular experience in these matters should decide what the punishments are to be. Witches should not be exiled as a punishment, because they will simply go away and then return to their congregations, and what's worse, they will infect others. However, those who are jailed permanently (who might be recidivists who have relapsed, infecting others and denying their case or retracting some point of their confession concerning themselves or others, for which reason they were handed over to secular justice) generally cannot infect others.

And note, reader, that generally in the case of witches, according to knowledgeable commentators, there are at the most only two diabolical illusions, [which are] produced through deception or by other means. [As concerns the first illusion,] the Devil sometimes gives [witches] money that appears to be real but is not (although the Devil sometimes gives them real money, as in the confession of Belotte Moucharde).[25] [Regarding the second illusion,] it sometimes concerns food, which appears to be other than it is, and sometimes they have in their congregations excellent and real food that is such as it appears to be. Furthermore, [the witches] do not stop meeting in the winter, for they celebrate even more than in warm weather, albeit without

25. Hansen notes (154) that "this Belotte was one of the three prostitutes who were first accused" in the wave of arrests resulting in the first Arras trial of May 1460. The names of the people arrested, tortured, and convicted or released in the Arras trials appear in other sources; the orthography (and even the names) vary greatly. For brief introductions to some of the other figures involved in the early trials, see below, nn. 57–58, 60–64.

fire. [They can do so] because the Devil adds some manner of heat quickly to the surrounding air such that the congregants do not suffer great cold, and their bodies are somehow warmed and heated by his food and by his heating up of their blood. It is sometimes even the case that these congregations have fire, by which they are heated through the skill and ministrations of the Devil.

[Methods of interrogating the accused]

The second thing to consider concerns the means of proceeding against any individual who has been provided with salutary admonitions and has sworn to tell the truth from the coming interrogations to the opening of his trial.[26] [It should be noted that] when interrogated, [such] an individual will lie repeatedly through the entire trial, and will make up many falsehoods—misrepresenting and denying persistently the crime of which he is accused—no matter how sincerely he has sworn to tell the truth. With great oaths and anathemas, he will then speak sweet and noble words [to the inquisitors]—while protesting, as one might expect, to the Devil: "Sire, ne te desplaise"[27] [Begging your lordship's pardon]. He will say that he will submit to an inquiry regarding his reputation, etc. All these things will be of little use to him, as will be clear in what follows.

He will cry out to God and the saints, especially the saint most frequently appealed to in his homeland, saying and begging that they should help him to the extent that he has merited. He will further say that he hates nothing more than witches, and wants them reduced to ash. However, those in attendance should in no way be moved on

26. The passage that follows offers particularly valuable insights into the ways in which the Arras prosecutors interrogated their victims. In the absence of the trial records, which were burned by order of the Parlement de Paris, this material helps us to re-create the specific steps they used—and the ways in which the accused "witches" responded to them.

27. This reference offers a glimpse at the ways in which the Arras inquisitors might have used the words and practices of the accused as grounds to prosecute them for imaginary crimes. As Du Clercq's *Mémoires* (4.4.25–26) suggest, Jean Tannoye, the "Abbot of Folly," regularly addressed these words to patrons at the end of his public recitations of poetry.

account of his words and his constancy, but rather they should imme-diately proceed to put him to the question, whatever he says. Nor are witnesses or accusers to be presented to him unless their good dispo-sition is known in advance. And furthermore, even if their good dis-position is known in advance, it is dangerous to confront [the accused] with them, as they might exchange signals by which, in the presence of the accused, they sometimes change [their testimony]. One can, however, ask him whether he is willing to confront witnesses, if it might help to speed things up; he will often say no, and that these persons are worthless, and that will be a sign that he is guilty. And if he says yes, he will not confront those whose evidence has already been heard, and time will be lost, as well as that session.

Then, indeed, when he is about to be put to the question, he will call on divine justice and say to those present that he cannot say what he does not know, and he will beg that someone should tell him what he should say. However, before he is put to the question, all of his clothes should be taken from him, he should be shaved and inspected in all his parts [and] his nails should be cut, in order to find signs of a pact, or any other small physical sign given by the Devil; or a hair, or a ring, or a thread, or anything else of that kind, the presence of which gives them [witches such as him] hope for the help and assistance of the Devil. As long as they have such a sign as a result of their covenant with the Devil, they will not confess, or if they do confess, they will immediately say that they did so by force of torture.

However, once the accusation or accusations have been examined by those in attendance using the aforesaid means, with due regard to every detail, and if after torture and interrogation he does not begin to confess on the spot, he should be "warmed up" and [admonished to] think carefully, and revived. And then, when he has been revived, and while the pain is fresh in his memory, he should be put to the question again, or put in a foul prison, and fed little and austerely. For the darkness of the prison and the lack and bad quality of the food will do much to make someone confess to his crimes, as will the harsh words spoken to him by some, and the gentle words of others, so that he will tell the truth.

And if he confesses to his crimes, those in attendance shall inter-rogate him about the place where he was, and about whom he coupled with; who was teaching, or spoke, or led; who presided, in what shape, and what his name was; where the ointments and the stick were (for first it must be confiscated from him); and about the gifts given by either side. [This should be done such that he tells] how it was, in conformity with the accusation. And all interrogations that are designed to elicit this kind of information should be conducted quickly (and those who are experienced in this kind of interrogation know about this from trials, and from this treatise).

Once he has confessed to having participated in three or four congregations or thereabouts—since in the beginning he will confess to having been at just one, even though he was there thousands of times, in order to distance himself from his crimes in hope of the mercy of the church—and once the places and times have been written down, [it will immediately be clear to] all in attendance that he participated in these congregations for a very long time. In general, the interrogation of accused parties should not follow a predetermined list of questions, which ought to be avoided scrupulously, and the names of all of those who are to be accused should be written down simply, and all at once, in this first interrogation, without details of the fornication and without disclosing the evidence.

When all these things have been written down as mentioned above, he should be questioned about the fornication, [in order to elicit] all the evidence, that is to say, the names, what people were wearing, etc., of both partners, for the sake of [ensuring] correspondence between all the accusations made or to be made by others. Finally, the interrogation should determine where, when, and at which of the aforesaid congregations they were, or whether they were at some and not at others. No one present should say anything by which they might be moved to excuse those whom they accuse or have accused—for some would seek nothing other than to excuse or to have an occasion to excuse the accused in obedience to the Devil,[28] thinking thereby to please those in attendance by their excuses—for they accuse [others] reluctantly and unwillingly, as will be suggested in greater detail below.

28. We have omitted the clause "et complaciensiam accusatorum" (and in order to gratify their accusers), which does not make sense in this context.

And note, reader, that they often do not wish to accuse anyone, thinking that they should not do so, or claiming that they had already confessed to a priest about the sect. For at the urging of the Devil, and of the people in their conventicles, they delay and are reluctant to accuse people of substance, and those who are not of their sort or status. Neither do they want to be the first to accuse their own friends or people of substance—saying on account of their own malice and that of the Devil, who very probably speaks through them, that in those congregations there are none but humble women and humble persons. For they believe or pretend to believe that they have been taught by the Devil and by their associates that they should not reveal the sins of others, or accuse others.

And in all these matters, those in attendance must be cautioned in advance. Remember, when the accused speak of themselves or of others, that if they anticipate their interrogation, and say that they know nothing about a matter about which they fear to be interrogated, then that is a sure sign that they know something about it. And understand, reader, that those who have been arrested recently have very likely been advised in their daily conventicles that they are to speak deliberately or with malice, naming or accusing all those whom their interrogators want them to name, or those whose [names] they think of first. And they do this in order to discredit and muddy the accusations, and every known fact, as, for example, when they falsely claim that an angel of Satan can transform himself into an angel of light and take on the form of men in their congregations, concerning which, see below, in a certain article, at length.

Nor, however, on that account, should the judges or those in attendance be influenced in any way; but they should listen to everything patiently, and to the extent that is possible use their good judgment to compensate and anticipate [further deception]—for there is no malice greater than that of the Devil and the witches. For it is to be noted that the witches often describe in their accusations, in many particulars, a person who is well known to them. [This may be] a person whose name they know, but whom they do not want to name because of their own malice and that of the Devil; or if they name him, they give him another name in order to confuse and muddy that accusation; or [they provide] one piece of evidence that has nothing to do with the person described. And often, either maliciously or by a conscious effort, they provide inconsistent information about a person's age more than about any other attributes.

And a man and wife can be members of this sect for the same reason or for different ones: the wife for carnal pleasures, the man for riches, or vice versa, or for some other reason altogether. For when someone has given himself to the Devil, practically all of the prohibited things he wants are allowed to him, and he is denied all honest and faithful things. A man can go to one congregation [and] his wife to another; and thus, sometimes, they do not know that the other is doing so, and sometimes they do know. However, coming together and being together in this sect has provided the occasion for some to join themselves together as though in matrimony. And sometimes a husband is a member of the sect and the wife not; and the wife notices nothing about her husband, for they go to their congregations in the darkest depths of night, when people are most likely to be asleep (usually after 11:00 P.M.), and they often return around the second or the third hour after midnight. Those in attendance [at the interrogation], or judges, should not be influenced at all if one man is accused of having been with a woman, and the same man is accused of having been with another woman, since this was in different congregations, and they go to many congregations, and for many more years than they confess. And sometimes even one man will have many women in the same congregation, and will go from one to the other. Indeed, the nature of the act is the same in all such accusations.

Finally, they are to be interrogated regarding harmful magic, and the questions should include how many people they taught and who those people were. And the trial should be held without interruption, if it is possible, and all in one sitting, for the entire trial should occur when they are disposed to speak the truth. For if it is deferred, those who have been released will be found, on another occasion, to have had their minds changed by the Devil or by other men. And note in particular, reader, that for the extirpation of this damned sect, those who conduct trials and inquisitions must focus especially on who ought to be accused and concentrate on further accusations of others, all the more so as regards the witchcraft perpetrated by these same witches. The whole point of persecuting this sect is that they will be effectively extirpated and exterminated, by the means of pointing out and accusing anyone whom they have recognized with certainty at their congregations. If this is not done, a large part of Christendom will be lost and the faith will perish.

2. HOW IDOLATROUS WITCHES ARE INTRODUCED TO THEIR SECT AND TAUGHT FOR THE FIRST TIME

Generally, they are introduced to the sect and the congregation not by a man but by a demon. When, for example, someone aspires from the greatness of his soul or for some other reason to some sort of difficult thing which is almost impossible to attain, he falls into desolation and despair; or when someone burns in the carnal lust of excessive, inordinate desire for someone else, he is thus liable to take any kind of forbidden action, or to succumb to the tumult of some disordered passion. The demon appears to such a desolate, desperate person, reminding him of his plight and promising a remedy if only he will obey him and surrender his soul—since the Devil does not do business otherwise. And then the demon takes him to the congregation and instructs and teaches him about everything, and gives him ointments and powders, the stick and everything, etc., if only he will consent to the Devil—for only consent without any reticence will suffice.

Very frequently, however, one man, once given the opportunity to speak, will teach another. He will propose to him—if he chooses to believe him—that he will improve his life, will obtain all desirable and desired things, will lack for nothing, and will see fine and wondrous things (and this can show up in trials [?]), especially if on a certain night—that is to say, if a congregation is about to be held—he wants to be transported outside the town in order to see that beautiful assembly; nor does such a man give a full account of all the details, or indeed of the way things really are.[29]

29. Our translation diverges here from that of Maxwell-Stuart (87): we insert a negative marker ("neque") that he appears to have missed.

Once the listener has given consent to all that, the instructor puts an ointment on a small piece of cloth or a piece of paper, and [gives him] a small stick to place between the thighs, announces the hour of the journey to the congregation, promising to take care of him at the hour of return, and to be there if he is not prevented; however, if he were to be held back, the instructor says that a certain man will come to take care of him. That man is a demon, who appears at the first congregations in human form and tells them to return, saying, "Such a man says such things to you, etc." On other occasions, at the approach of night and the appointed time, the instructor and his familiar demon often appear in the guise of animals. The demon tells him how, on a certain day, a particular person had spoken with him. And the crowd of people going out for the first time [leave] either by some secret path, or through the window, or through the chimney. Because of the thickness of their bodies, the walls of the chimney or its parts are suddenly separated by the work of the Devil, and then rejoined—imperceptibly to us—for the Devil works wonders [against the order of nature]. We know this because of his [ability to] open any sort of closed or locked thing.

[As they exit,] bent over with anointed sticks placed between their thighs, they say, "Va de par le dyable, va" [Go, by the Devil, go!] or "Sathan, n'oublye pas ta mamye" [Satan, don't forget your lover!] or some such thing, and then they are raised at great speed to the lowest part of the middle region of the air, which is exceedingly cold (and from which they suffer pain in the heart and in the breast, and even their eyes suffer from the violent and sudden parting of the air, especially when they fly for a long time, even though the demon provides them with some protection and prophylactic). And they are fearful—especially when they go a long way—perceiving the great distance and the places over which they are flying.

Indeed, the novices are warned not to think of God and the saints, and they are reminded that they must not sign themselves with the cross—otherwise, they will fall. When they reach their destination, they do the things described in the following chapter. When these things have been done and finished, replacing those same anointed sticks [between their thighs] as they did previously, they return to whichever place they wish—or the demon wills. They keep the sticks between their thighs the entire way, going and returning. And note, reader, that the demon sometimes appears to them in visible form for the entire journey to the initial gatherings; but more often, he carries them to their meetings without being visible. And sometimes one stick is enough for two people, and the instructor and the novice fly to the assembly and return from it together.

3. HOW THE INITIAL GATHERING AND "SYNAGOGUE"[30] ARE CONDUCTED

When a woman is introduced for the first time to the gathering (and the same is true for a man), by a demonic caretaker or familiar according to his custom, as well as by a man or a woman who introduces friends whom she knows to the congregation, she is presented to the presiding demon—who always appears in masculine form—although the names and forms or faces [of the others] appear as men and brute beasts conjured up in various forms. Sometimes there is more than one presiding demon. If, however, such a woman presented in this way is of vile condition and low status, the presiding demon—father of arrogance—hardly will deign to speak, saying that such a miserable woman is unworthy to be received at that gathering because she would not be able (the presiding demon says, his voice hoarse, when he begins to speak, after a certain delay) to perpetrate any notable crime or great evil in the world at the order of the said presiding demon.

If, however, at length the woman is received into the congregation through the intervention of her demonic caretaker, and of her human instructor, she renounces God and Christ, the glorious Virgin, all the saints and the suffrage and protection of the saints, Holy Mother Church, and the sacraments. She abjures the faith completely, promising most particularly not to go to church, not to sprinkle holy water over herself in the sight of men, unless it is to deceive them (while saying [to the Devil] under her breath, "Sire, ne te desplaise" [Begging

---

30. This usage reproduces both scriptural and inquisitorial practice of using terms related to Judaism to describe diabolical or heretical opponents.

your lordship's pardon]); not to make confession to anyone, unless fictitiously; and especially not to confess anything about this damned sect. Nor is she to look at the consecrated host elevated in the hands of the priest—which the presiding demon calls a filthy idol—without making the protestation, "Sire, ne te desplaise," [uttered while] spitting on the ground in disrespect, if it will not be seen by those around her. The presiding demon even permits her to throw holy water behind herself or on the ground, and to trample it with her feet. And the demon also orders a cross to be made on the ground, then covered in spittle and scuffed or desecrated with the feet in contempt of Christ. And he teaches [the novice], moreover, to make an imperfect [sign of the] cross by knocking herself under the chin. He even orders the body of Christ to be brought by someone thus [newly] received to the congregation and sullied and trampled upon by those present. And in particular contempt of the great teacher of the world—as the presiding demon says—the novice bares her backside and shows her nether parts to the heavens.

When these things have been done as described, she adores the Devil on her knees, and makes homage, kissing first his hand or foot with the offering of one candle of black wax as his due, [which is] usually given to her by the familiar demon called N., or with the offering of some money. When that candle has been received by the presiding demon or by those around him, it is put out. After that, the presiding demon turns around. The woman who has been received kisses the presiding demon's posterior, and then she gives her soul to him to have when she dies, although she swears most solemnly not to reveal this in court. And indeed, those who are of this sect confess this rarely and unwillingly. For the Devil never, as we have already noted, negotiates or makes a pact—especially in any clear way—unless he receives the soul as a pledge. Then, as a sign of this gift, the Devil receives a *wadium*[31]—such as her finger, hairs, or fingernails, and very

---

31. Niermeyer's *Mediae Latinitatis Lexicon Minus* (Leiden: Brill, 1976, vol. 2) defines a *wadium* as "a pledge; an object which in a symbolic way binds a person or his property (the debtor) who, in consequence of an unlawful act or contract, has assumed obligations toward the opposite party (the creditor)" (1458).

frequently some amount of her blood—since (as Augustine says) the Devil loves spilled human blood.

And, in return, the Devil first gives—by way of recompense— some grace or special faculty, or the promise of money, which he sometimes provides (since he knows the location of hidden treasures and he always has at least some [of them] at hand, by the just permission of God, and since, by that same permission, he is a great thief and knows very clever ways to oppress poor people through rapine, usury, and such deliberate exactions).[32] Or he offers the ability to use women or men for pleasure, or to heal quickly by superstitious means. The Devil himself sometimes accomplishes such healing (supposing always the just permission of God), working quickly, in a hidden way and imperceptibly. [He is allowed to do this] on account of the infidelity and sins of those who are to be healed, who have engaged themselves unwisely, rejecting God and human help, thus endangering their souls. He provides them with seeds of corporeal matter, either by breath and the attraction of the air, or in food and drink, or by some secret conduit, bestowing health on the body, or removing blockages. For sometimes a body, when cured in this way, was already at the point of being cured, and so it got better anyway. The Devil did not make it happen, although he could have foreseen it by a clever guess. For the Devil very frequently deceives and lies when he makes promises; for he is a liar and the father of lies.[33] Yet he sometimes knows means that can be used for healing.

He may instead empower those who are in the grip of hatred to avenge themselves, offering the rod of vengeance, which brings certain death [to their enemies]. With God's permission, the Devil himself consigns both good and evil men wherever he pleases to death,

32. The discussion that follows is an extended meditation on the power of demons to act in the real world—an important debate in Scholastic demonology during this period. See above, pp. 9, 17. For an equivalent discussion in Tinctor's *Invectives,* see "The things

that demons do in reality" (pp. 125–30 below).

33. Our interpretation diverges here from that of Maxwell-Stuart (89), who reads "mendax est et pater eius" as "he is a liar and so is his father."

through the use of toxic and lethal elements, by the same means stated above that he uses to bestow health. Sometimes he fails to deliver on his promises, either having lied deliberately or because God does not permit it; and sometimes, like a diviner, he predicts that death will come from a natural cause or from some other cause that he has cleverly guessed, without causing that death himself. Or the Devil grants [these people] the special ability to reveal hidden, lost, or invisible things, and to recover hidden treasure, or the power to resist four or five assailants, or to attack and defeat the same number. Or [he may bestow] the faculty of pre-announcing and predicting the future beyond the common ability of human beings, especially as regards the state of the weather—when it will snow, or when the air will be calm, or when it will rain, or when it will hail, or when there will be thunder and storms, etc.

Often the Devil speeds these things up, and with God's permission, calls up and quickly produces clouds and other materials by local motion. By divine permission he can move and transport objects[34] of the created order to produce these effects seemingly in an instant, in order to keep people in his damnable sect, and make them place their hope steadfastly in him, [such that they believe] that he will certainly fulfill his promises—someday. This often happens because the Devil is a liar, and is deceptive and mendacious; he cannot do anything unless God permits it. God sometimes does not permit [him to accomplish] small things, yet in other cases allows [him to accomplish] major things. Thus the Devil deceives people, and fails to fulfill the things they expect and hope for. For the most part, however, the clouds are arranged randomly, in accordance with the way things normally happen, and they produce whatever effects they are going to produce at any given moment.

In addition, he bestows the power and the strange and extraordinary abilities to attain offices of secular power and lordship, or dignities and benefices in the church, by fawning and simony, so as to

---

34. Here, Maxwell-Stuart (90) has translated "ex sua creatione" and "transmutare" in grammatically plausi-ble ways that are, however, inconsistent with Scholastic demonology.

amass riches, or to achieve other damnable ends. Or he promises the power of remaining in the good graces of magnates and princes, or of great men, by means of love powders or potions, which he gives to his people so that they can obtain from those princes whatever is asked, and can control them, or can achieve other goals, on which more below. For the Devil, in this case, affects the souls of lords indirectly, one after the other [after the fact?], acting upon their blood and humors and placing stimulants in their food, or [employing] the means touched on above, in order to arouse their senses and to provoke passionate affection toward those for whom he is working—or he bestows some similar kind of power.

Moreover, beyond the various powers listed above, the presiding demon then gives to such women received into the congregation some tangible token—such as a ring of gold, of copper, or of silver, or a thread, or a roll of paper showing unknown letters, or some such thing—by the touch or use of which some effect that provides the special power that has been granted [to her] is caused. For he usually promises to a woman received [into the congregation]—beyond the two special gifts noted above—all goods in abundance, and promises never to be absent or to stay away, especially if she invokes him when in need. In fact, however, he usually does not appear when she needs him, for he is mendacious and deceitful, and God's justice does not permit him always to be present. Nor is [the Devil] there to help in particular when such a person is about to be arrested by the authorities, nor does he help even when she has been arrested. For such a person, the Devil can do nothing on these occasions, though sometimes he might appear to prisoners in visible form and speak to them. And take note, reader, that the Devil, when called, frequently appears to the witches while they are free, in order to keep them in the sect—and frequently he goes to them without having been called. Hence all witches, although they always deny it, are Devil invokers.

Thereupon, following the form of a sermon more or less, he persuades the novice and others present at any congregation, that no matter what scholars and preachers say, they are liars and they preach falsely to the world; that there is no other god other than their prince

Lucifer, who is the higher god,[35] and that they themselves are gods and immortals. However, [he tells them,] the souls of men die with their bodies, as in the case of dogs or any sort of brute beast. Nor is there after death any hot or cold place, or delights or afflictions, paradise or hell;[36] but the only paradise is what he shows them in their congregations, that is to say, where all pleasures are to be had for a nod, and men in each congregation go promiscuously from woman to woman.[37] And the same thing happens to women who are present in the congregations, where they feast and are pleasured, and they lack for nothing that they need.

After he has said these things, the presiding demon rises from his seat, which is elevated somewhat above the earth before the others and situated at the head of the congregation. He then withdraws and takes the novice to some part of the forest, in order to embrace her in his way and know her carnally. He says cruelly that he will throw her on the ground on her face, on her two hands and feet, as he cannot copulate with her otherwise. And no matter which form the presiding demon has adopted, when the novice first touches his member, she finds it cold and soft, as his whole body often is. He first enters the natural opening and leaves corrupt and yellow sperm, harvested from nocturnal emissions or in other ways, then [he enters] the place of discharge [the rectum], and thus he abuses her unnaturally, by which deed such a novice commits a sin against nature with the Devil.

And then the presiding demon returns to his seat, and the woman returns to sit on the ground with other men and women sitting not in a circle but in large rings,[38] some sitting face to face, some sitting back to back, and some back to face. And that woman sometimes goes to *tripudia*[39] that are held there, just as in the real world, though with greater excesses, and she is truly and really there, not in her dreams

35. Maxwell-Stuart reads "Luciferum, qui summus est deus," as "Lucifer, who is god on high" (91).

36. This may reflect inquisitorial anxieties about contemporary forms of Epicureanism.

37. The Anonymous may be giving voice to ecclesiastical concerns about the subversive potential of sexual behavior.

38. Here, we follow Maxwell-Stuart (91n93) in reading "ringas" or "rengas" in lieu of "reugas," which appears in Hansen's transcription of the Latin text.

39. As Maxwell-Stuart notes, the *tripudium* was "a ritual dance consisting of three steps forward and one back" (91n94).

and fantasies,[40] and she is present in body and in soul, and the same thing can be said about the others who are present: living men participate consciously, playing stringed instruments, drums, and other instruments, just as cooks are sometimes there to prepare food. And such a woman, before taking refreshment, engages in carnal copulation with some other men, or she stays in her seat until she has taken her fill of refreshments.

If the presiding demon touches the earth or a tree with his stick, there will sometimes be found tablecloths there on the ground; in fact, they have been placed there at some point by men on their way to the congregation, or by demons. And there are copious amounts of meat and fish there, and often the roast meat of calves, red and white wine in earthenware vessels and cups, and in earthenware jugs and pots. They feast splendidly and they enjoy themselves, sometimes to excess, around the table, each man and his female neighbor telling each other stories intimately. And similarly the demons—although this is rare—pretend and seem to eat, though the regulars present know well enough by what deviltry they eat. And note, reader, that there are three types of food there—or so it seems—and the same can be said of the drinks; [first,] the best food there is brought by demons after they have received it from witches in their own homes or it is furtively gathered and transported there by demons with the permission of God; [the second is] real food, to all appearances, brought by the witches on their way to the congregation. The third [type of] food is different from what it appears to be owing to a bewitching of the eyes, as for instance demons sometimes give real money, and sometimes give things that are other than they appear to be. In this case, the demons cause beer or water to appear to be wine, and similarly regarding meat and fish.

And indeed, frequently when they dine, their table servants are male and female demons in great number. Once the meal is over, if there are candles, they are extinguished, and by the order of the

---

40. This is a clear reference to the canon *Episcopi* and to the ongoing Scholastic debate over the reality of night flight and witchcraft (see above, pp. 9, 17). Note that the Anonymous takes a different (less nuanced) position on this issue than does Tinctor, who suggests that the accused witches may be imagining these events (see "A notice to judges," pp. 138–39 below).

presiding demon, each one does his due, and each man takes his
woman aside and knows her carnally; and indeed unspeakable
excesses are committed in swapping women by the order of the
presiding demon, and in going from woman to woman and from man
to man in abuses against nature of women with one another and
similarly of men with one another, or of women with men outside
the proper orifice and in other parts. The witches enjoy themselves
even more there, and feel greater ardor of lust, than [they do] in the
real world, because the Devil inflames their body, and [because]
demons place powder and other stimulants in [their] food and drink
to inflame and heat up their carnal desire, so that the more they mix
with one another voluptuously and licentiously, the more they are
enticed and inclined to continue in their congregations. And yet a
man never experiences delight with a she-devil, or a woman with a
demon, but consents to copulate out of fear and obedience.

Then they go back to their *tripudia,* and when it is done, the
presiding demon reminds the congregation of his orders and restric-
tions, touched upon above, with others that will be listed below,
saying that if they obey his commands, they will never lack for anything desirable and necessary, nor will they be captured by the authorities. And if not, it will go differently for them, and he offers an
example: "A certain N. of the congregation was arrested because he[41]
did not obey me in any and all things," and if some people are burned
by the authorities and placed on the path of salvation, which is
extremely rare, he says that they died because they did not obey his
commands. And then he thunders terribly at them, threatening them
with death unless they carefully obey his commands; and if they die
a natural death on the path of perdition, or they die impenitent, as
often happens, he speaks of their death with more moderation, almost
happily.

And after that, he returns to the previous commandments, and
then adds a further list:

• First, that they do not confess, or that they not speak with priests,
  as noted above.

41. As Maxwell-Stuart notes, "N. is
designated masculine in the Latin text"
(93n96).

- Second, that they not speak to each other about this sect in the real world, but that they conceal it entirely.

- Third, that they declare publicly that these things are dreams and fantasies, so that the authorities will not be alerted to them.[42]

- Fourth, if the authorities arrest some [of them], and recognize the reality and truth [of their activities]—that is, they do not overlook them or permit them to go away unpunished—those who were not arrested will foment rumors and clamor among the people, for the purpose of ensuring that [those arrested] are burned quickly. This is to prevent them from accusing others, and so that the Devil will all the more quickly drag the souls of those who have been captured down to hell, and cast them away, which he is waiting to do.

- Fifth, he most especially orders that if they are captured by the authorities, they should be ready and choose to die rather than to accuse any one of their accomplices; and if they obey these things, the Devil himself will help them avoid death, and they [must] promise the Devil and the other accomplices of the congregation most strenuously to fulfill this.

- Sixth, that they instruct and lead to the congregation as many as they are able to in order that they acquire a greater [number] for the demons; otherwise, they will be whipped as severely as they are when they fail to obey [his] other commands. For sometimes they report heavy beatings by the demons with the sinews of cows or being stabbed with awls or by sticks that the Devil keeps close at hand.

- Seventh, that as noted above, they never confess to having given their soul to the Devil.

- Eighth, that they come back frequently and that they return willingly to the congregations as often as the latter are announced to them.

- Ninth, that they not be present where witches are burned.

---

42. This "commandment" calls to mind the 1453 trial of Guillaume Adeline, a theologian who was charged with involvement in diabolical witchcraft on the grounds of having argued against the reality of the Sabbath. On the Adeline trial, see Martine Ostorero, "Un prédicateur au cachot: Guillaume Adeline et le sabbat," *Médiévales* 44 (Spring 2003): 73–96.

- Tenth, that they promise they will do nothing to reveal their acts of wicked magic in a law court or anywhere else.

And then he announces the time and the place of the next congregation. When all of this is finished, as described above, saying good-bye to the presiding demon, they return to their own places, sometimes on foot if they are close. But often they mount on their anointed sticks or rods or stocks, and return very rapidly, transported by the Devil through the lowest portion of the middle region of the air. And note, reader, that on account of the violence and speed of motion, even after having taken good refreshments, they very often suffer hunger during their return.

This may also result from the great bodily exertion and agitation and expenditure of energy in the act of sex, and from dancing after eating. It may also result from traveling through extremely cold places when the natural heat of the body is drawn into a single place within it—for the sake of digestion via antiperistasis[43] and because they [the witches] are so exposed to the surrounding cold.

Then, the second time the novice attends, she is known carnally by her familiar demon and guide, as she was previously known by the presiding demon. [But] the demon does not have sex with her at subsequent congregations, except on those occasions when there are not enough men to make up couples (since there are generally more women than men). At such times, the demons take the place of men in the couples, just as on those rare occasions when women are scarcer, demonesses make up the lack.

This is how events unfold in other congregations after the first two meetings. During the first of [these meetings], when coming back from meeting the presiding demon, after having been received into the congregation, [a male new to the sect][44] is known carnally by a demoness, who takes him to one side before he is seated with the

---

43. "Antiperistasis" is a classical philosophical concept that was adopted by some Scholastic thinkers. It refers to processes by which qualities such as heat and cold are intensified when exposed to their opposites. In this case, exposure to cold air is thought to cause witches to experience higher internal body temperatures.

44. We follow Maxwell-Stuart here in supplying this implied subject, which appears to be missing from the manuscript (94n97).

others, and in the second, in a similar fashion after the offering brought by everyone at each congregation, he is known by a demoness. However, it is sometimes to be noted, though rarely, that a man has a demoness on top of him,[45] and this is a sign of great wickedness in him. And similarly, a woman will always have, in every congregation, a man or a demon.

And note that in that territory or region, some congregation is celebrated practically every night—sometimes on the same night in various forests and places—although not every person of the sect in that region goes every single night to a congregation. Those who go less frequently go to a congregation at least every fifteen days, and sometimes they go to other localities and far distant regions. Indeed, on festival evenings—as occurred last year on the vigil of Saint Martin[46] in the winter—there were, or could be, in one and the same place at different times (or at the same time in many places) a number of congregations presided over by demons, such as first at the wood at Neufvireille,[47] then in the congregation of Guillaume Tonnoire[48] in the form of a black man, and then in [the wood] at Tabary[49] in the form of a dog and of a number of bulls, etc., and this is how these women and men travel, vagabonding from congregation to congregation. The congregations are held at night, generally after eleven o'clock; daytime congregations are not as frequent, although they are celebrated at all times of the year, during the day and the night.

[Participants] are carried by demons through the heights of the air to those meetings that are far away, and returned likewise. They are rarely carried in this way to those [meetings] that are close by, although they sometimes are; but they are not seen, either because of a veil interposed by the demon (just as the congregations are sometimes not seen at night by passersby, although they are sometimes

---

45. That is, he takes the forbidden passive position. Maxwell-Stuart reads the odd locution "vir . . . superhabet dyabolam" as suggesting that the man was on top of the demoness (94), which does not make sense either grammatically or as a special form of wickedness.

46. As Maxwell-Stuart notes (98n99), this refers to Martinmas, which takes place on November 11.

47. "One of the many places called Neuviller [Neufvireille] that cannot be determined more precisely." Hansen, 164.

48. We have not been able to identify this individual.

49. "This place cannot be found." Hansen, 164.

heard) or because of the wondrous speed of their movement. However, anyone who were to be present at the point of their departure—should anyone be there—would be able to see them; but they return from a secret place, where there is no one else around except the Devil, who is visible to them and not to anyone else. Those who are close [to a congregation] frequently go and return on foot by day. And note here that the demons have common names according to the [fashion of] names of the men of each region where they live.

From the preceding matters, apart from the evil deeds described below and the many perjuries before judges when under examination (for they do not care about perjury and making themselves anathema and swearing falsely), it is clear that these witches, by their own fundamental and formal admission and reception into the congregation, are apostates from the faith, idolatrous and guilty of the crime of divine *lèse-majesté;* that they have an express pact with the Devil and with a familiar demon; that they are invokers of demons; and that they act immorally, against nature, with demons in varying shapes of men and beasts. And sometimes,[50] moreover, if they bring others to the congregation—as they promise and indeed do—it is clear that the authors and principals of this dreadful, damnable sect of idolatrous witches are, then, arch-idolaters. Furthermore, it is clear that all the witches commit the same and equal wickedness in each congregation, for they have one and the same form of profession and a similar type of behavior in their congregations in each region—though outside the congregations, some do more evil deeds than others, either because they have been witches for a longer time or because they are more given over to the Devil and forsaken by God.

4. CONCERNING THE EVIL DEEDS THAT ARE COMMONLY DONE BY THE WITCHES IN OBEDIENCE TO THE COMMAND OF THE DEVIL

The witches sometimes work together to accomplish the evil deeds that they wish to do, and they always obey [the Devil], specifically for

---

50. As Maxwell-Stuart suggests, "interdum esse" should be read here instead of "interdum sese" (95n101).

fear of him. It is fear that subjects them to him once and for all, for the Devil acts as an agent of divine justice. And so they are incited by their human instructor to commit many wicked deeds. Indeed, they burn down houses and estates, and everywhere they set fire to [the houses of] men both known and unknown to them, and those of the good and the bad alike. God permits this to test the patience of the good, or for some other reason unknown to us, and known only to him. At the prompting of the Devil, they do great and frequent damage to good lands—to the vines, the grain fields and the meadows, etc., of men known and unknown to them, casting forth with the wind certain powders given to them by the Devil or by their human instructor, or made by them, as appears in the trials. And when these powders have been cast forth—either because the clouds [are] naturally disposed to cause such an effect and are summoned by the action of the Devil through local motion, or [because] the Devil causes a cloudy substance to arise and appear in the blink of an eye—there appear from the clouds whirlwinds scattering hail and frost, or some type of storm, and consequently the fruits of the land are ruined and desiccated.

They collect consecrated hosts at Easter time, or on other days, having pretended to confess, with a great show of signs of devotion. Coming to the altar table [to receive communion] at masses which they have paid for, they take the host out of their mouth under the cover of a napkin [and place it] into their other hand and then into their sleeve. They take it back to their home, in order to give it to toads, which they nurture in earthen pots for use in making their ointments with certain other ingredients, as described in the trials. These ointments are meant to procure transport to the congregation—not that these ointments have the power of transporting men, but at the order of the Devil, men stoop to such wickedness that they give their Creator, Savior, and Redemptor God contemptuously to one of the most vile and abominable creatures that is known to man.

And thus the Devil leads men to such execrable sacrilege, and to carry out such great crimes. For after they have had [the toads] consume consecrated hosts while hungry, they extract blood from them to mix up a bloody potion. Afterward they burn and pulverize the toads themselves for the same purpose, so that one of them should have the means to instruct another how to do this. For it is that same

Devil who, sometimes visible to men—but rarely—transports them during the entire journey to the congregations, and often remains invisible along the entire way, though he might be visible on their return. The anointed branches or sticks have no power to carry people, but they are held to have the capacity to do so, so that when people have come together in agreement [to practice witchcraft], one man may have a means to instruct another and to lead him into the synagogue and congregation, and so that the Devil might operate in greater secrecy and transport men under the cover of these visible outward forms.

They obtain revenge and cause the death of those they hate using the [anointed] rod of retribution, or using something else given to them by the demon, as described above. Midwives especially, when they are of this sect, kill many infants before baptism by strangling them, etc., just as priests, when they belong to this sect, commit many abuses of the sacraments of the church. For male and female witches do the same, either by driving pins or needles into the brain, or by squeezing [the infants'] tender members, or by other reliable means, such as extracting blood from recently and secretly exhumed corpses, by cutting open their stomach, or by some other means, in order to make their compounded ointments, etc. And sometimes they take the bodies of roasted infants to the congregation in order for them to be eaten,[51] as appears in some trials (especially from the region of the Lyonnais)[52], or they roast infants at the congregations. They do many acts of sorcery and evil magic and enchantments using love powders or potions, or love infusions[53] given to them by the Devil, or a piece

---

51. As noted above (p. 7), accusations of ritualistic cannibalism and infanticide are some of the oldest components of the elaborated theory of witchcraft. They date back to late antiquity, when they were leveled at groups of early Christians and other marginalized groups. See Cohn, *Europe's Inner Demons*, 1–15.

52. We consider Maxwell-Stuart's identification of "Leiden" here (97) to be erroneous. While "Lugdunensis" may be read as the genitive "of Leiden," the *Orbis Latinus* reveals that the term is also a standing expression referring

to the Lyonnais region of Burgundy (see http://www.columbia.edu/acis/ets/Graesse/orblatl.html). Our reading seems correct, given that a group of witchcraft persecutions were believed to have occurred in the Lyonnais (as attested in the contemporary treatise "La Vauderye de Lyonnois en Brief").

53. The Latin *houppellos* is derived from the Middle French *houppelet*, which refers to something like a bag full of spices or herbs to make an infusion of some kind. This was probably similar to the pouch referred to in modern French as a *bouquet garni*.

of cake,[54] or some such thing, and they also cause many poisonings. They poison wells and rivers by means similar enough, and in brief, they cause innumerable great scandalous deeds that cannot be related at length in this paper, but it is not necessary to describe all their deeds.

5. ON THE DIFFERENCES AMONG WITCHES CONCERNING THEIR OPINIONS ABOUT PARADISE AND HELL AND THE IMMORTALITY OF THE HUMAN SOUL

Some witches confess that there is an immortal soul and paradise and hell that are eternal, but many other sins that are grave are not sins in their false opinion. Thus they claim not to sin in going to the congregation and doing the things they do there, especially because their forefathers, who, they believe, were of good reputation according to the standards of the day, did such things and passed them down to them. Others agree with the presiding demon that the human soul dies with the body, and that there is no paradise or hell, etc.[55] And if they are interrogated and maintain this position in their answers, or are resolute, they are to be considered heretics.

Yet others believe, like the first group, in the immortal soul, paradise, and hell, but [are] impenitent, without hope, obstinate, hardened, and indifferent to salvation, although they know that they sin most gravely. It is enough for them that as long as they live, they enjoy their pleasures and live deliciously, voluptuously, and selfishly. And they say that if they do not go to one place, that is to say, to paradise, they will go to the other. A fourth group believe that the soul is immortal, paradise exists as well as hell, and that they sin gravely, yet however at the end, before death, they hope to repent and confess. However, they are deceived, since witches are often overtaken by death like other people are, or they are too late in making provision [to become righteous].

---

54. "Gastellum nicart." Niermeyer (*MLL*, 1976, vol. 2) defines *gastellum* as cake (1130); the *Dictionnaire du Moyen Français* (http://atilf.atilf.fr) notes that *nicart* is synonymous with *écart*, meaning "piece."

55. An Epicurean position; see above.

6. ON PUTTING ACCUSED WITCHES TO THE QUESTION AND TORTURE

Questioning starts with pleasant admonitions and gentle exhortations, etc., in keeping with the law and with reason. If the accused constantly deny their deeds under oath and perjure themselves, as they almost always do, it would be irresponsible not to put them to the question or to torture them. Torture is generally the only way to get anything out of them. Neglecting to torture them extinguishes and buries crimes, hiding them and keeping them under wraps, and openly favors the Devil, in contempt of the living and true God. Moreover, it [omitting torture] would openly encourage this damnable sect; [for] it is extremely secretive and hidden, as appears from the above. Nor can demons of this sort be expelled without torture and judicial questioning.

And anyone who stops harsh torture and questioning in this matter ("harsh" meaning everything short of death, mutilation, or the loss or ruining of members, for this is an unusually grave crime) is most strongly to be suspected of belonging to this sect, aside from the fact that they are trying to impede the duties of the Inquisition (for which reason they are to be considered excommunicate). Such people probably are afraid of being accused and are implicitly trying to protect themselves before they are accused.[56] By excusing themselves, therefore, they are clearly accusing themselves. For the unique nature of this crime necessitates unique torments.

During the process of torture and judicial questioning, a unique battle is being fought—not principally against a human being, but

---

56. Chilling allegations made during the appeals before the Parlement de Paris suggest that this accusation was used to increase the length and severity of torture employed in the Arras prosecutions. The king's advocate, Jean Simon, claimed that while Nicole Gavrelle, a prostitute and suspected *vaudoise*, was being tortured, her jailer spoke up on her behalf. "And when the jailer said that she had had enough of this, [her torturer] told him that he [too, i.e., the jailer,] was a *vaudois*, [and] that he would have him burned and would do it himself." Archives nationales X/2a/28, fol. 391r–v, transcribed in Franck Mercier, "L'enfer du décor: La Vauderie d'Arras (1459–1491) ou l'émergence contrariée d'une nouvelle souveraineté autour des Ducs Valois de Bourgogne" (PhD diss., Université de Lyon, 2001), 585.

against the Devil, who has great power over the witches who have been justly forsaken by God, for they unjustly deserted their God and Creator, etc. It is the Devil who suggests and implants responses as though he were speaking through them; just as the apostles, when they spoke before kings and princes after the Holy Spirit was sent to them in tongues of fire, were spoken through by the Holy Spirit. The Devil, moreover, who is sometimes visible to those being questioned, but not visible to those present, or is invisible to both, impedes the tongue, the throat, and other members that form the voice, by diverting and redirecting them [the tongue, the throat, and the other members], sometimes tangibly and visibly to those present. The Devil helps them powerfully (since he has a wondrous power over them) as they are practically completely his, and he stops them from speaking lest he lose his prey via the complete confession of their crime.

[He] also [helps them to avoid] accusing others, especially people of higher social rank, who can do greater villainies in obedience to the Devil, and who, by their authority and ability to act, [are most able] to promote this damned sect. The true value and benefit of these matters—and the best opportunity [for getting confessions]—arises chiefly and principally in accusing more important people, since punishing some miserable and lowly men or women, as far as the benefits of that are concerned, is of use merely to warn the faithful of that estate or similar class not to join this sect. Nor then are witches of the same status, or greater, really capable of correction because of the nature of this damned sect, for once they have given [themselves] [to the sect], they cannot withdraw on account of their fear of the Devil and his threats, for they do not come back to the bosom of the church on their own, except most rarely and, essentially, miraculously, unless they are captured by the authorities.

Witches generally hold out until the end, by recanting or otherwise, no matter where they end up. This crime is extremely unusual; for that reason, almost all these things which concern this crime are unusual, and not to be found in any other sort of crime whatsoever. But if the more important people are left alone, the Devil will ascribe it to his own intervention [i.e., he will be encouraged]. And the witches will attribute this help to the Devil, on account of which they will follow him all the more tenaciously, lead more people to the sect, perpetrate worse ills, and thus, with the passage of time, greatly augment this most nefarious sect.

7. ON THE VALUE OF WITCHES' OWN ACCUSATIONS OF OTHERS

Assuming [that the following conditions are met], accusations [against other alleged witches] are always to be taken seriously:

(a) that [those made] not only under torture, but also without torture, are confirmed and ratified, and that they [the accusations] came entirely from those same witches when they were testifying without anything having been placed in their mouth by tendentious interrogation or otherwise, which must be avoided—for nothing predetermined should be asked of them or placed in their mouth; and

(b) that the persons accused have been charged by proper procedure, and based on many details concerning the place and the time and evidence (and designating and naming the parties among the accused people, together with the evidence, adds a great deal to the value of such accusations).

Nor, as one hears from those with the most experience and sees in the pertinent treatises, is it common to find in this matter (as one so often does [in other cases]) slanderous accusations arising from hatred of the persons accused, or from some other wild passion, etc.

Sensible judges can discover this from inquisition and interrogation, for they accuse only the guilty in the sect, for reasons that will be adduced immediately in the following. A recent example was the *Abbé de peu de sens* [Abbot of Folly],[57] who, as he claimed, hated and was hated by only one man, an inhabitant of Tournai, who had taken his wife from him twenty-two years before, and although he would

---

57. A reference to Jean Tannoye, known by the nickname the "Abbot of Folly," which appears to be related to his membership in a *confrérie joyeuse* (see below). On the textual error in the original Latin, see Hansen, 169.

have preferred that other one to die rather than himself, he always said that he [the other man] was not of this sect, nor would he accuse him of being one. This sort of thing can be found in trials and confessions of witches concerning others. For such accusations—the aforementioned premises remaining the same—are very significant, and have great force, even more than those concerning their carnal unions, for the witches are [normally] extremely reticent about making accusations, and they always do it unwillingly, and understate their accusations.

Nor if they are held for an entire year will they accuse everyone whom they know, nor will they state the entirety of their crime, such that they knowingly keep a great deal about themselves and about others quiet, to their own damnation; and they would rather choose to confess their own crime and die than to accuse others, remaining in this greatly and damnably loyal to the Devil and to their associates. We have the recent example of Houtmelle, alias Lechat,[58] who in the absence of torture confessed his deeds of his own free will, and when questioned harshly in order that he might accuse others, did not want to accuse anyone, when it is very likely that he knew many members of the sect. And thus one finds daily the same difficulties in other cases as regards accusing others. They are very sparing in accusing others, first of all because of the most peculiar promise they made to the presiding demon and to other accomplices in the congregation, and second, to others, not merely in their congregation, but in the everyday world, not to accuse anyone.

And they are reluctant, furthermore, to accuse others on account of the great friendship that they have contracted with them, which is based on kinship, or of the great benefits they have received without making any return, or because they associate with each other daily, or have had sex together, etc. In particular, they [do not accuse] others of high standing, in case accusing them, as the Devil suggests, might cause their own death; for [they fear] that they would incite threats

58. Hansen notes, "In the margin, in the same hand: 'Hotmelle *dit* Lechat'" (169). This probably refers to Jean Lefebvre, a member of the first of three groups of accused *vaudois* to be tried in Arras. He died in prison under suspicious circumstances (see the introduction, n. 3). His nickname was "the Cat."

from other men, or perhaps they think it likely if they were to accuse
[their social superiors], they [the accusers] would come to the notice
[of their social superiors]; or they [do not accuse people of higher
social standing] because of the hope and prospect of assistance [from
them] in escaping death.[59] For they think that they will have to get
along with them in the world, and hope to do so, and they hope to
return to the congregation. This shows how much they fear the Devil
and [these] men, and how much they are influenced by them on
account of the fulfillment of their desires, etc., in that sect.

Another reason is that the Devil impedes them from making
accusations in the way detailed above in the immediately preceding
article, in order that he not lose his prey. In particular, he impedes
witches from accusing people of the higher orders, whose obedience
to him leads them to commit greater evils. Furthermore, for these
reasons, accusations against people of the higher orders are more
vehement and of greater force than those against people of lesser
orders, even though, on the other hand, judges should pay more
attention to important and highly placed people than to low and vile
ones. Nor does the Devil care much if witches who have confessed
their crimes die. Indeed, he rather prefers their rapid death, so that
he receives their souls; but on account of the great subtlety, malice,
and power that he has over them, he stops them from accusing anyone
other than those who are already imprisoned or some few other people of their sect and station.

To solve this problem, therefore, zealous men of good judgment
who are experienced in this peculiar matter may—on the basis of one
single well-founded accusation and taking into account the particulars
of the case—imprison, question, etc., vile and low persons in particular, as noted above, and this will not invalidate the case. We have
recently witnessed here the cases of Deniseta,[60] who was accused only

---

59. We have read this passage
according to the social hierarchy of
the time.

60. Deniselle/Denisette Grenier, a
prostitute, was the first person arrested

in the Vauderie d'Arras. She was tried in
the first of the three trials that took place
in 1460. She was handed over to secular
authorities in Douai, her hometown, and
was executed there shortly after the trial.

once, of the abbot,[61] of Coleta de Le Strebee,[62] of Ieremia d'Auvergne,[63] of Belota Moucharde,[64] and of a number of others. And the extraordinary nature of these cases is always to be kept in mind, for only those who are guilty can be witnesses or make accusations, on account of the hiddenness of this matter, because it is extremely secret. It is necessary when the witches confess and accuse others to ensure that everything is recorded in writing, especially [the testimony of] all people accused based on the circumstances and evidence of both parties to copulation, for the sake of agreement and concordance between these and other accusations.

Nor must the interrogators say anything from which those being interrogated might construct an occasion to excuse others, because, on account of the influence of the Devil and the promises made to him, they are prone to excuse others, and they seek nothing other than to excuse [them], for those reasons, as above. And they are to be listened to after they have started to confess; both their confessions and their accusations of others should be heard informally, without officials present, to the extent possible. When they are being questioned, only one person should speak and interrogate them at a given time, for witches who are being interrogated very much like either to speak vaguely—avoiding the matter at hand—or to address a larger group. When they accuse others or confess, [only] a few men—honest ones

61. As Hansen notes (170), this refers to "the above-named *Abbé de peu de sens*, Jean Lavite," a.k.a. Jean Tannoye. Tannoye was a traveling poet and musician and a member of a *confrérie joyeuse*. He was the second person accused in Arras, and was convicted and executed at the first trial, in May 1460.

62. According to Du Clercq, Colette Lescrevée/Lescrebée, a prostitute, was among the second wave of people arrested in Arras; she was executed on July 7, 1460. Among the group of prisoners with whom she was publicly chastised, Colette distinguished herself by steadfastly refusing to confirm the crimes to which she had con-

fessed under torture. See Du Clercq, *Mémoires*, 4.8.36–39.

63. Jeanne (Iohanna, *not* Ieremia) d'Auvergne, a.k.a. la grosse Jeanne (Fat Jean), the madam of the brothel in which all of the prostitutes charged in the Arras trials (except Deniselle Grenier) worked. She too was arrested, and was tried and executed in May 1460.

64. Belotte ("Cutie") Moucharde, a prostitute, was a member of the first group of suspects arrested in Arras. As noted above, Moucharde managed to escape the fate of the other prisoners executed in May 1460; she was sentenced by the local Inquisition to go on pilgrimage.

of good intentions—should be present, for they [the witches] are shy of crowds, or of new and unknown men, or of their friends, whom they might otherwise accuse.

And when they begin to confess their crimes, and to accuse [others], they should be examined diligently about those crimes and accusations, all in one session if possible; for otherwise it will later be found that the Devil or other men have induced them to recant or change their minds, if proper care has not been taken regarding the prisons. For the jailor, if he is well disposed to his work and is a virtuous and honest man, can do a great deal of good in leading him or them [one or more witches] to a true confession of their crimes and in eliciting accusations of others. If he [the jailor] is bad, it is very prejudicial, [for] when he visits them, takes them out, takes them back, or gives them the necessities of life, [he can] either encourage them gently to confess the truth or discourage them from telling the truth, or encourage them to recant things they have previously confessed.

And understand, reader, that no accusations of others can be hoped for or expected when [witches] are about to die, especially since when on the point of death, witches unjustly exonerate those whom they previously had accused, in obedience to the Devil. Good and serious men will regard such excuses as null and void. For when they are at the point of death, witches have often made a particular commitment to the Devil (in accordance with the instigation and promises touched on earlier in the discussion regarding all promises made to him). [They have promised] to act, for the sake of achieving things I will describe below, in such a way—for example, by acting in an unjust manner—as to die in a state of mortal sin, disputing and denying their crimes, saying that they said everything only because they were forced to under torture, etc.

8. [ON THE POSSIBILITY THAT DEMONS MIGHT IMPERSONATE INNOCENT PEOPLE]

Accusations made by witches concerning their accomplices are not to be dismissed merely because some people say that demons present at the witches' congregations can represent and impersonate innocent individuals who are ignorant of this matter and who have never had anything to do with this sect. The first reason [not to dismiss such accusations] is that witches who frequent congregations do not accuse demons, such as the presiding demon and the familiar demons or serving demons, appearing in human form and serving at table, or sitting at the head of the group with others, though they know them by name. Nor do men make strong accusations against people otherwise unknown to them, whom they see in the congregation without knowing their names; therefore they accuse only those whom they know to be human beings, and who are known to them other than merely by having been seen by them in the congregation.

For when they accuse them with an exact description, it follows not only that they have seen them in the congregation, but that they must already have seen them in the world, because otherwise they would accuse everyone from the congregation. When they accuse them by name, they know them not only from seeing them at a meeting or in the world, but also from having listened to them or spoken with them or about them. And sometimes [they know them] through carnal copulation in the world, or in the congregation, or in both. Or [they know them] through some conversation and familiarity with them in the world or the congregation, or because they led them for the first time to the sect and congregation, or were led by them; for the instructor and the novice often go to the congregation together, and come back from the congregation together.

The second reason is that such witches make very definite accusations against individuals whom they know only from the congregation when they know their names and towns, where they are from, etc., from hearing [them], speaking [with them], or associating [with them], and they do not accuse demons whom they know only from the congregation by name from hearing [them], speaking [with them], or associating [with them] when they appear in human form in the congregation. Therefore, it is significant that they accuse only human beings, and that they truly and certainly discern and distinguish between human beings and demons, between men and [male] demons, [and] between women and she-devils, as will clearly appear below.

[Arguments against exculpating defendants on these grounds]

If those who try to dismiss the accusations by witches made about other accomplices provide examples—for there are many in books—let them quote the book and passage where these examples first and originally appeared, so that it can be seen why and to what end they are citing them, along with other considerations and accompanying circumstances. And when, with the grace of God, a sufficient reason and appropriate response is provided in regard to any such example to satisfy any questioner, everyone will see clearly that these inquiries have no bearing on the congregations of the witches. [And therefore, there is no reason to] dismiss [such accusations] on account of these examples, or to minimize accusations made by witches against their accomplices.

For demons, in some cases, can appear in the form of human beings in order to deceive them (God permitting). Learned men, particularly those well versed in holy scriptures, are aware of [how this is done]; and the illustrious doctors treat this [topic] at length in their books. In particular, that venerable doctor Saint Thomas Aquinas [does so] at great length in the first part of his *Summa*.[65] But in the matter of witches, and in cases concerning them, the possibility that demons take on the appearance and form of men does not have standing among learned, prudent, and good judges; therefore, one need not invalidate the accusations of accomplices made by witches, based on the material above, and as the following will more amply illuminate.

And indeed, this is easy to see from the confessions and trials of witches, since witches distinctly know and can discern real and true men from demons, and demonesses from women. If such an impersonation were to occur there [at the congregation], therefore, the men and women in attendance would detect it. And the present writer has never seen or heard any witches among those who have been questioned who would not be capable of clearly and distinctly recognizing the difference, on the basis of numerous signs, between a true woman and a demoness, and likewise between a man and a demon.[66]

There may be those who want to invoke precedents of the supposed impersonation of human beings by demons of both sexes in

---

65. As Maxwell-Stuart notes (103 n114), this may refer to *ST* I, Q. 114, Art. 4.

66. Another clue that the author was present during the interrogations.

such congregations. Such people are unlearned in letters and less suited to speak on such matters. Aside from the fact that they must fear that speaking with malicious intent about such things, of which they are ignorant, would incur their excommunication (since this, on its own, is to impede the Office of the Holy Inquisition and its outcome), they would also undermine, impinge upon, and err implicitly against the article of faith "The Holy Catholic Church," etc.[67] They should remain and believe in all obedience, humility, and fear, and piety of faith, and bind their intellect in obedience to faith, and acquiesce to the judgment and disposition of the holy church.

For the Catholic Church, on account of these congregations of witches in many Christian lands, and on account of the enormous crimes committed in such meetings or resulting from them, rightly states that both men and women are to be punished, justly and rationally. Moreover, the church (which cannot be mistaken, as it is led by the Holy Spirit, and by the infallible rule, especially in those matters which touch faith) proceeds against those accused [witches], in order that such people [who would invoke precedents about impersonation] should take their cue from those who have heard witches speaking and who conduct their trials.

If indeed such people, citing examples, think themselves learned, let them observe with their own eyes, on the one hand, the confessions and trials of witches; let them hear them speaking, and let them weigh everything on the scales of discretion and true and correct judgment; and on the other hand, let them look up in the primary and original documents these alleged examples along with all the relevant circumstances concerning the possibility of impersonation, as above, and secondly, [let them look up] the treatises and books of the doctors, especially the treatise *De discrecione spirituum*[68] and its contents. If

---

67. Maxwell-Stuart notes that this refers to the 1302 papal bull *Unam Sanctam* (104n115). Issued by Boniface VIII in the context of a struggle with secular authorities, the bull argues for the necessity of submission to the church. See http://www.fordham.edu/halsall/source/B8-unam.asp.

68. This may refer to a treatise written by the German theologian Henry of

Langenstein (ca. 1325–1397), *De discretione spirituum* (*The Discernment of Spirits*). On Henry's contribution to contemporary debates over the problem of discernment—that is, assessing influences and actions of spiritual beings—see Wendy Love Anderson, *The Discernment of Spirits: Assessing Visions and Visionaries in the Late Middle Ages* (Tübingen: Mohr Siebeck, 2011), 159–89.

they know what is good for them [if they are reasonable], they will be silent, and they will place a guard upon their mouth, and all around their mouth and their lips.[69] And if they attempt to maintain their opinion obstinately and unreasonably, they should be judged in the same way as unlearned people have been in the past, and it will be easy for a man well versed in holy scripture and experienced in these matters to satisfy them fully and to [provide] answers regarding this matter to anyone who asks.

Note, however, reader, that very often those who allege such examples in these matters—according to the writings of the most important treatise writers and men of practical experience—either are accomplices in the sect of witches or have been corrupted and led to allege these things by accomplices. These accomplices know with certainty the truth that they deny, even though previously, with cunning and malice aforethought, they said that they were dreams and fantasies. But now, finally unnerved and refuted by the clear truth, they take refuge in saying that the angel Satan can transform himself into an angel of light. For in those congregations, as is amply clear from the trials and confessions of the witches, demons and demonesses are present. But to say that there are no men or women there is to fall into inconsistency and to be contrary to the article [of faith] "Our Holy Mother, the Catholic Church, etc.," as noted above.[70]

For it is furthermore audacious to declare something that anyone is unable to know unless it is revealed to him. And it is, moreover, irrational and unintelligible to say that demons appear to one another in both sexes in assumed bodies for any reason other than to deceive people, especially when no humans are present. It is clear, however, that real live humans of both sexes are present there, as the trials and confessions of those same witches demonstrate. For no one who is alive, unless he were a witch with experience [of these matters]—or had seen the documents of confessions and trials of witches (or their copies in books)—would know how to concoct and invent any such confession of the sort that any illiterate witch makes. And such a

---

69. As Maxwell-Stuart notes (104n117), this is a reference to Ps. 140:3 (in the Vulgate; Ps. 141:3 in the KJV).

70. The author is referring to *Unam Sanctam*; see n. 67 above.

person cannot truly say that some men and women are actually and personally present in those congregations, and others are impersonated by demons, unless he is one of the accomplices, or unless it has been revealed to him.

Nor can it be reasonably believed that God would permit some innocent people to be represented [as members of] this sect by demons in order that they be punished as though they were members of the sect. Indeed, if such a case is to be believed, [it must also be] piously believed that God would reveal the truth to the judges, or would inspire them to discern it, lest an innocent individual be punished as [a member] of the sect. And moreover, in this case or in any case where it should happen to be thus, judges would determine with certainty and with due forethought—based on the confessions of witches and their trials, and all the surrounding evidence of those trials—that there were demons and demonesses in those congregations, and not merely innocent individuals impersonated by them.

[How witches discern demons]

For as follows from the above, witches who frequent such congregations can truly tell the difference between a woman and a demoness, no matter which woman the demoness might impersonate, and similarly between a man and a demon. For everyone who accused Iohanna[71] d'Auvergne testified that in the seat beside her was her sexual partner, who was always a male demon, and that Iohanna confessed that she had copulated only with a male demon in those congregations. And similarly in other trials, other witches testify that demonesses and demons have sometimes been part of such fornicating couples, distinguishing between men and demons, and between women and demonesses. And note, reader, that accepting this as true, even if it is possible (unless it were already established), would be to undermine the entire truth of this matter and to block any and all useful outcome that could follow from this. For the same thing would

71. Referred to above (incorrectly) as Ieremia; see n. 63.

apply to any men when they were impersonated by demons, or could be thus impersonated; and therefore, either no one was impersonated or all were impersonated, both of which are unlikely, as is clear enough from the above.

Nor can it be said that in these congregations there are really and truly men and women only of vile and inferior status, and not of solid and high standing, or that the latter are necessarily impersonated by demons. For sometimes some are of solid standing—according to the standards of the time and the mistaken estimation of men—who are less consistent in reason and more apt to be deceived and induced into this sect, for some reason, than those who are of lower status. Nor do human judgment and public opinion, which are often unreliable and false, or even seemingly proper behavior that shows outward signs of piety, or any such things, have any bearing on the matter of witches, because they hide the crime that is most secret and exceptional in nature. However, they ought to be considered at least in part, and weighed by the judges. For given that it is commonly and correctly believed that men of high and solid status are more rational and more consistent, and less inclined and less given by their nature to vices, there is, however, another way to make the pact more enticing. For the demon assails them all the more in order to overcome them and bring them to the sect, and he rejoices to receive them, as is clear from the trial of magister Guillelmus Adeline,[72] and he refuses and disdains to receive vile persons into the congregation, for he is the father of arrogance.

Thus the witches know, by the four senses, the one interior (that is to say, by force of thought or assessment), and the three exterior senses (that is to say, by sight, by hearing, and by touch, especially in embraces and fornication), and even sometimes by scent or odor and by the intellect and by many other signs which would be too numerous to adduce here, how to distinguish demons from men and demonesses from women, and thus, consequently, how to tell the difference between a real woman and one impersonated by a demoness, if such a one were to be present. And they can tell the difference between a

72. On the Adeline trial, see above,
n. 42.

man and a demon via their intellect or assessment, for witches are terrified by the sight of demons in whichever sex they appear, however much they are used to seeing demons, for they usually have a terrifying face and their physical form and movements are clumsy.

And by that same power of thought, they infer that what they see is hostile, just as a sheep, at the sight of a wolf, flees. [They distinguish demons] by sight, for the demon forms the body that he takes on from condensed air or other things in such a way that one always sees signs in that body by which the demon is recognized, either from the black color always imposed upon the imperfect type of humanity or in a body not well finished in solid and firm shape, or often by its excessive size. [And they are known] by their speech or by their strange conversation and manner, by not eating very much at all, or sometimes, by how they pretend to eat, although they do not really eat, just as they do not perform the functions of living beings, such as real and living men do, who in these congregations exercise all the functions of life, and speak intimately with one another.

[And demons can be recognized] furthermore by their arrogant manner and infrequent speech. They are especially and certainly recognized by sight by those who frequent the congregations because demons generally have big eyes, and in such congregations their eyes are always wondrous, terrifying, harsh, fiery, enflamed, shining, sparkling, etc. [They can be recognized] by the sound of their unclear voice, which is hoarse, as though they were speaking into a pot, or a jug, or a trumpet. [They can be recognized] by touch because their body is generally soft and frigid, or in some other way differently constituted than a real and living human body; and it is especially easy to recognize them by touch in carnal copulation, as the trial records reveal, as all learned judges of good faith, and particularly those with real experience in this matter, understand. For a woman has no or little pleasure in carnal embraces with a demon, but submits to the demon out of fear and obedience, and he deposits a material that is very frigid and humid, corrupt, yellowed, etc. With a real man, she has the same pleasure in the congregations as they have in the real world—or more, as is apparent from the above.

[They are] sometimes [known by] scent or odor, for a body assumed by a demon on rare occasions can be the body of a dead person, but most often it is formed from fetid, condensed air, or the demon quickly and imperceptibly forms a body in this way using some fetid material. [They can be recognized] by the intellect, however, because witches are finally left by their dealings with demons desolate and sad on their return, and the intellect notes this desolation and sadness; therefore accusations based on sight are reliable, and those based on hearing and sight are even more so, and those based on touch, especially in carnal embraces, including sight and sound, are the most certain, and most forceful, and have the greatest weight.

The same thing can be said when the accusation is made by a novice who is being instructed, or when an instructor is teaching a novice, and one of them accuses the other. Accusations also reinforce each other and are verified[73] when made by one of the parties to fornication when [accompanied by] all the details of their clothing and other circumstances of place and time regarding the fornicating parties, and especially when one or the other of the fornicating parties confesses.

And to conclude: if all or many of the accomplices have been captured, they themselves, and all their supporters, will desist from insulting and opposing the truth; however, when anyone should want either to object against what he said previously or to propose some example or other, let him identify, as above, the chapter and verse, and with the guidance of Christ, he will be given a particular answer to any argument or precedent, such that any honest man should be content with it.

And note, reader, that if the examples that can be adduced regarding the transfiguration of demons, or the possibility that humans might be impersonated by demons, can be used and have some role in undermining the accusations against congregations of witches, then by the same token, in the case of manifest crimes such as theft, homicide, adultery, and other crimes of that kind, malefactors and accomplices could not be convicted from the testimony of witnesses,

---

73. We adopt Maxwell-Stuart's emendation of "rubor" to "robur" (107n121).

since the malefactors would allege that demons had taken their place, because they can transfigure themselves, etc.

9. ON [THE WITCHES'] REVOCATION AND DENIAL OF THEIR CRIMES AND THEIR ACCUSATIONS OF OTHERS, AFTER [THEY HAVE MADE THESE] CONFESSIONS AND ACCUSATIONS

If, in a proper trial, held according to best practices, after [witches] have begun to testify in their own words (without anything having been put in their mouths) before an inquisitor and in the presence of judges, etc., or of clerks and a notary or notaries, once the confession of their crime and the accusations of others are found to be true, especially without torture (or if they are first tortured, then [once they affirm their confession] without torture)—if, for some other reason, when they are visited in another legal action at some later date, they revoke their confession, retract and deny both their crime and their accusations of others, they make themselves unworthy of the grace and mercy of their church, especially if they do not reaffirm their previous confession in its entirety regarding themselves and others, for they are to be treated, should they not completely reaffirm their original confession, in the same way as pertinacious heretics, who are to be given over to secular justice without mercy.

And if they do not return immediately to the things that have been said and set down, both in this section [article 9] and the one concerning the value of an accusation, as above [article 7], the judges should not then be moved by their denial and revocation; on the contrary, both an accusation or a confession about oneself and accusations made of anyone else [should be treated as being] of equal value and weight as if [the accused] had always persevered in their confession and in their accusations of others. Otherwise, no reliable and firm judgment could be made about them, nor would it be possible to proceed against those accused, and all would revoke their confessions, and no one would be punished; it would be a useless, never-ending, and vain enterprise to try to proceed on such grounds if they were constantly changing their confession and revoking it.

Should they revoke, retract, and deny everything, especially on their deathbed, despite having been under the care of priests of the highest quality and great discretion—exculpating and excusing others for the sake of obeying and pleasing the Devil, who moves them to do so, as touched on below—they would die without due process, and justice would have to be put off, etc. No one could be tried on the basis of accusations that the witches have made and later revoked, for [the accused] would say that none of [the accusations] were [made in] sound mind and good judgment. Nor might one say that [those so accused] could be justly punished, notwithstanding their revocation; nor might one say that their accusations of others carry no weight. [In such a situation,] it would be impossible to pursue a case against either group, for the same principle applies to both. [The cases against] both sides could be disqualified in the same way, for the principle applies as much to one group as to the other.

But it is also the case that they could have decided, before they were captured by the authorities, that if they were arrested and confessed, [they would] immediately revoke [their confession] on their own or by the advice of the Devil or of an accomplice, with no one else suggesting a revocation, or for any other reason. However, it is probable and more credible that these revocations arise from a lack of proper supervision, and from the suggestion or instigation of accomplices or of accused persons who have not yet been captured, [either] in person or by intermediaries, or by letters, or by some other means, by which everything is exposed and brought to light. [They will do this either] because they fear to be accused, etc., or because they want to muddy the matter and cause scandal, etc., or [because] accusations are procured by the jail keepers, who are afraid or have some ambition for themselves or for their friends, or who are moved by some inordinate passion. And for that reason, particular care must be taken with prisons, for if the incarcerated are well supervised and are treated to sweet and gentle exhortations, it is not to be doubted that once they have made their confession, they will stick to it.

And it is to be feared that those imprisoned will already have promised, in order to create confusion and scandal, and to protect others, that when they are on the point of dying, they will excuse those whom they have accused, and say of themselves and of others that they said everything under duress. Upright judges must not trouble themselves about this, as noted above. Rather, wise and discreet priests should be assigned [to the prison]; they should share a common understanding of this thing or matter, and be well disposed, and [should not be] influenced by accomplices; [priests] should hear [the witches'] confessions, and [should] lead them and bring them to justice. Other, new priests should not be employed to deal with them at this time.

For they generally revoke and deny or retract things that they have previously confessed for three reasons. The first is on account of the fear of death, which they think will be quite soon, and by this type of denial they hope to evade death or put it off. The second is for the sake of those whom they have accused, for they think that this type of denial will render accusations they have previously made against others null and void, although they are of as much value as if they had persevered in the things they previously said, just as exculpations of others are not to be accepted after a first confession without torture, etc., on account of the tendency they have to exculpate [others], and on account of corruption by simpleminded accomplices and suggestions made by the Devil or by men, etc.

The third is mainly, indeed, [that they fear] that things might be required of them beyond the preceding confession of whatever concerns themselves or others, that would strengthen the case against them or [their] accusations of others whom they accused unwillingly, thinking to themselves that the judges would be content with their return to their prior confession without further interrogation. And sometimes the sign of the pact given to them by the Devil has not yet been erased, and if at that time, after they have revoked their confession, they ask for a confessor, it would not be a good idea to give them one, since what they will confess then will be entirely harmless and laughable, just as their confessions usually are. Nor are their oaths to be believed at that time, for the same reason, when they swear that they are not guilty, or that these people or those people have been falsely accused, etc.

And note, reader, that they are to be brought back to their prior confession, first by friendly admonitions and gentle exhortations, and second, either by inquiring who told them that they should confess thus and thus, anything or any particular thing regarding their prior confession, or by isolating [their confession] into separate parts and assisting them by asking about things not included in their prior confession. And one should say that that confession was true, praising the person for the truth of what he had said previously, even though it had not contained everything. Or [one could proceed] by threats, and by showing them the instruments of torture if necessary. After they have reaffirmed their confession, they should be asked why they revoked it, and who persuaded them, and then, if the judges do not intend to ask further questions, they are once again to be arrested; otherwise, the trial would go on forever, etc.—neverending trial.

10. ON JAILS AND ON THE INCARCERATED

The greatest care and caution is to be taken in law regarding prisons. It should be ensured that all guards and other people who work in the prisons are faithful and honest, and well disposed to this matter, [and are] not under suspicion, etc. Those imprisoned should not communicate with one another, and outside accomplices or other accused people should not have access to the prison, either in person or by intermediaries, or by letters. Everything should be kept secret; otherwise, many problems will ensue, especially if accusations of others should be revealed. For there might even arise, among other things, a conspiracy and an attempt to cause some kind of harm to the judges or to others who are involved in the matter. And note, reader, that it is likely that those held in prisons for good reasons—if they do not receive comfort and daily news or hope via communication from outside while in prison, or if they are shown the darkest corner of the prison (where they would have to live a miserable existence) or are transferred to some other town—will perhaps confess their crimes. And it is a given that, should they never confess their crime, they should not go free with impunity if they are accused for good reasons.

11. [ON THE RETRACTION OF CONFESSIONS AT THE POINT OF DEATH]

Any priests may minister to the witches regarding the denial and retraction of confessions, especially at the point of death. It is not to be wondered at if the witches deny their crimes at [this] point, appealing from the judges to the divine tribunal[74] and saying that they confessed by force and are being put to death without cause, invoking the sweet name of Jesus, and calling upon the saints, etc., and [claiming] that they sincerely believe that they were never witches. Thus they want to exculpate others before they die. And when there are great rabbis[75] in the sect, they proffer the following words: "But Jesus, passing through the midst of them, went his way,"[76] as is well known by many experts and written in treatises.

If witches lie sick in their bed for many days or months, and are not held by the authorities, and by some kind of miracle, on their own, touched by God, confess at the beginning of their sickness the entire truth about this sect and its reality with its wicked magic—yet because the Devil lies in wait for the heel of man [Gen. 49:17], that is to say, ready to devour souls at the end and in death, at the point of death having called a priest, they deny, at the suggestion of the Devil, the reality and truth of this sect previously confessed by them, they become liars and their confession no longer is whole. And they say

74. Our reading diverges here from that of Maxwell-Stuart ("calling for divine judgment on their judges," 111); we read "appelantes de iudicibus ad divinum iudicium" to mean "appealing from the judges to the divine tribunal."

75. Continuing the analogy to Judaism and "synagogues." See the introduction, n. 37.

76. A reference, as Maxwell-Stuart notes (111n125), to Luke 4:30, an account of Jesus's early mission. Members of a synagogue in Galilee, upset by Jesus's preaching, seek to throw him to his death, but he leaves them peacefully

in this manner. The Anonymous seems to suggest here that the "witches'" cynically appeal to the very Christian tradition that they are abandoning, and that they seek to depict their prosecutors as a hostile mob. It is worth noting that the chronicler Jacques du Clercq attributes these very words to the "Abbot of Folly" in the moments before his death (*Mémoires*, 4.4.25). For an insightful study of this passage, see Matthew Champion, "Symbolic Conflict and Ritual Agency at the Vauderie d'Arras," *Cultural History* 3 (April 2014): 1–26 (esp. 11–15).

that they were dreaming, and that what they confessed earlier was not true.

And the same is often found among witches who are condemned to perpetual imprisonment: when they die in jail, they revoke everything in this way, just as other witches often do at the point of death. [They revoke their confession] first in contempt of the fact that they are about to die; and sometimes, perhaps, they have been led to hope in the grace and mercy of the church during their interrogation, and so they hope not to die. Second, [they act] under the influence of the Devil, who imparts to their imagination, and therefore to their intellect, the mistaken idea that if they deny everything, they will not be put to death, but will be brought back by the secular authorities to their town. Thus they are made into liars, perjurers, [and] excommunicates, and they commit mortal sin. Justice, however, is not deceived, and they die in that perilous state. Furthermore, they might not have confessed everything their judges inquired about regarding themselves and others, but knowingly concealed much, nor confessed completely, except perhaps in their own heart. And if sometimes they show contrition by tears or other outward signs, they do so solely on account of the fear of bodily death, and in order to escape it, or on account of worldly honor.

And the third reason—especially when the matter is new to a people, and there are thought to be many accomplices—is that the Devil suggests that they deny their crime to stir up the people to riot with their accomplices against the judges and their officials, who would seem to have condemned innocent people, especially when those about to die use such fine words when they choose at the end to be put to death in their denial.[77] For [this is done] in order that other accomplices not be prosecuted, and in order that those who are held in prison be liberated and justice not be done, and that those in attendance believe that [these things are] dreams and fantasies, and in order that the Devil not lose others or any other of his prey, but [that they] continue to obey him in order to do evil.

---

77. This claim seems to reflect the actual circumstances of the Arras trials; the accused were executed following protestations of innocence.

Nor is it wrong if witches are thus left rightly to their death, for particularly during their lifetime they merited it, unjustly leaving God for long portions of their life; for God is just, and such a life leads one to such a death; and especially when, during their reception into the sect and the congregation, they gave their soul to the Devil to take after their death. And although they can be broken, and may confess to giving up their soul, and are thus not incapable of penance, yet generally they do not confess or abase themselves regarding this in particular, but they die impenitent, obstinate, obdurate, not having confessed fully as witches, or they are put to death in prison, either by the hand of justice or any way they can.[78] For the signs of their contrition are most often false, [made/done] in order to evade bodily death or the destruction of their worldly honor, etc. And it is likely enough that at the point of death, the Devil appears to them visibly in order to terrify them and to lead them by his suggestion to undermine and deny that which they had previously confessed, in such a way that they should say that they confessed by force and in order to exculpate themselves and their accomplices.

12. HOW THE WITCHES WERE RIGHTFULLY HANDED OVER TO SECULAR JUSTICE [FOR PUNISHMENT] WHEN THE FIRST SENTENCE WAS RENDERED HERE, AS THE TRIAL RECORDS SHOW

First they were turned over to make an example, that is to say, to give an example to the people, and thus to edify them; second, on account of the novelty [of this thing], which was first recognized here [in Arras]; and third, on account of the extremely grave nature of this matter in and of itself, and the huge number of accomplices.

And although it is true that the church should be merciful and gracious, nor should it close its bosom to those returning to it for the first time, it must be known that when someone returns to the church

---

78. This seems to refer to Jean Lefebvre, who was found dead in his cell before the first trial (see above, n. 58).

on his own, by his own will and his own decision, and with complete sincerity in a way that can be seen by exterior signs, then, indeed, [the authorities] should be merciful—especially if such a person, who returns [to the church], did not commit homicide or damage the lands of others or commit any of these sorts of wicked magic, or was given over by the church to secular justice bearing the burden of having committed wicked magic. When, however, cases of repeat offenses are credibly believed to be more worthy of grace and mercy, or are more forgivable than [those of] many of their accomplices, [either] the church can in this case put off imparting mercy and [put off] receiving into grace those who offend more than once, or it can extend mercy [to them], while [nonetheless] not giving grace on the first occasion or at the time of a first judgment being executed.

For indeed, when someone returns to the church by force, and not with a whole heart, appearing to be impenitent, showing only false and simulated rather than true signs of contrition, and has been a member of the sect for a long time, and refuses to admit everything that he knows about the crime when he is asked, and is reasonably believed by the judges [not to have told the entire truth] regarding himself and others, and when he has taught many or introduced them to the sect, the mercy of the church can be justly denied to such a person, even on a first offense.

This is what happened in the case of the first six [witches] to be condemned. And finally, after many other signs of their impenitence—which the judges took note of—many, in their impenitence, and in confirmation of the aforesaid signs, denied their crimes even unto their death. Two women of their number acknowledged their crimes to the secular authorities and were given over to the ecclesiastical authorities for investigation, namely, because, beyond being members of the sect of idolatrous witches, they had committed sins[79] against nature, abusing [their bodies] with demons in human form and in the shape of various brute animals. And they performed sorcery and created illusions [using] powders given to them by demons, and [using] certain other mixtures. And they acknowledged all of

---

79. The list of "sins" that follows reiterates many of the key elements of the elaborated theory of diabolical witchcraft. See the introduction.

these things before the ecclesiastical court, and [admitted] that they had a familiar demon and an express pact with the Devil, in keeping with the [customs] of the witches' sect.

The other four, both women and men, however, collaborated with those two in all of the aforementioned wicked deeds, and furthermore committed many acts of wicked magic and sacrileges with consecrated hosts given to toads, and caused damage to good lands, and led many to this damned sect of witches, in addition to[80] committing many other crimes, etc. And one, a certain Denisetta,[81] perpetrated child murder, and the "Abbot of Folly" killed many men. And all the above things are proven to be true by the judgment and by proceedings of the trials, etc.

13. A BRIEF EXHORTATION TO THE JUDGES

Regarding this most infamous sect of witches, therefore, which has been growing rapidly in recent times and is most injurious to the common good, [and which] remained hidden in the folds of the earth and the corners of the woods as though it were not there at all, for many years in this region through the assistance of the enemy of humankind: God is to be implored by the constant prayers of the faithful to now arise and disperse his enemies so that those who hate him flee from his face.[82] Thus, those who write about such great matters—and the judges, under the aegis of Christ, whose cause is at stake—may gather, by the prayers of those faithful people, each and every one, and cooperate, working with their Creator to get to the crux of the matter. Thus God himself will be exalted, and his highest honor restored. For it has been usurped by the savage Prince of Darkness, in his arrogance, ambition, and iniquity, since days of old.

Therefore, let the judges now remember how faint and how perfunctory and momentary this mortal life is, and how fleeting are all the pleasures of this world. Let mortals consider in this spirit that it

---

80. We adopt Maxwell-Stuart's addition of "non" before "absque" (113n130).
81. Deniselle Grenier (see above).

82. As Maxwell-Stuart notes (114n142), this refers to Ps. 67:2 (in the Vulgate; Psalm 68:1 in the KJV).

is proper, beautiful, laudable, and meritorious to engage the Devil one-on-one in combat for the faith of Christ and God. And [let them consider] how divine and close to saintly it is to give honor to the eternal living and true God, especially when he shows himself powerful by means of such solid building material for virtue—the building material of eternal happiness and salvation, where the harvest is great continuously, and which requires many hands.

Let them consider carefully to themselves for days and years whether they have, in so many things, led by worldly fear or human favor or some other sinister motivation, closed their eyes and pretended not to notice and neglected to punish and rectify so great and such unheard-of wickedness and vice against God and Christ, now that the need is clear. For when they appear in that tremendous Day of Judgment before the strict and just judge Christ to such great confusion of their souls, they will receive for their dissimulation and neglect eternal damnation with the Devil and his angels. But if they act with all zeal in such matters of faith honestly, virtuously, ardently, and diligently, keeping God before their eyes, it is doubtless that they will finally be carried up by the eternal God for such divine deeds to the blessed seats of heaven, and they will have the greatest pleasures through all the ages. *Amen.*

Here ends the lecture about the witches at Arras.

A CONTEMPORARY NOTE ON THE MANUSCRIPT

One of the two manuscripts in which the *Recollectio* appears (BnF MS lat. 3446) appends to the text a lengthy note reflecting on the scriptural and theological basis for inquisitors' claims concerning alleged witches. While, as Hansen notes, the note is written in the same hand as the text of the treatise, there is no reason to assume that the author was the Anonymous of Arras. He was, however, a contemporary of the Anonymous, and, like the authors of both of our treatises, he was interested in the contemporary debate over the extent to which demons can effect change in the real world—including the question of whether they can move human bodies. The text of the note is as follows.

A note on the authorities regarding the matter of witches

[GREGORY THE GREAT, *MORALIA IN JOB*]

Gregory, in the fourteenth book of the *Moralia in Job*,[83] says the following concerning this statement of Job, "His troops come together, and raise up their way against me":[84] Malignant spirits unceasingly pant to harm us; but, although they have a depraved will of their own, they do not have the power of harming unless the highest will permits it. And though indeed they unjustly try to harm us, they are not allowed to harm anyone unless justly permitted by God, just as those who have abandoned the yoke of God have caused their own downfall by serving them [demons].[85] So [writes Gregory] in this passage.

A GLOSS ON 1 CORINTHIANS

"We should not lust after evil things, as they also lusted.[86] Neither be ye idolaters, as were some of them. As it is written, 'The people sat down to eat and drink, and rose up to play.'[87] Neither let us commit fornication, as some of them committed, and in one day, three and twenty thousand fell [died]. Neither let us tempt Christ, as some of them also tempted, and were destroyed," etc.

The gloss: These sins of a people moving away from God signify the substance and order of a weak people relapsing into sin. For they are first moved by evil lust. Second, via lust, they choose idolatry, which does not prohibit lust, in order that they might cultivate it [lust] and [worship] idols at the same time, just as the weak of Corinth did. And after they had lapsed into idolatry, they fell into acts of bodily pleasure. And after they were tempted into fleshly pleasures, they despaired of eternal life, which is to tempt God and to doubt his power.

83. Pope Gregory I (ca. 540–604 C.E.), known as Gregory the Great, was one of the four "doctors" of the early medieval Latin church. His thirty-five-book *Moralia in Job* (*Morals on the Book of Job*), a commentary written between 578 and 595 C.E., was one of his most influential works.

84. Job 19:12 (KJV).

85. This is a paraphrase of parts of *Moralia in Job* 2.3.14.46. For a full version in translation, see http://www.lectionarycentral.com/Gregory Moralia/Book14.html.

86. The passage that follows is 1 Cor. 10:6–9. We could not identify the "glossator" cited below.

87. Here, the passage in Corinthians refers to Exod. 32:6.

And then, finally, at the end, they became rebels against the faith, and they fell into those things that [Paul] earlier said were done; here he [Paul] says "they fell into them." In them were guilt and punishment, and in both was the prefiguration of our guilt, that is to say, our future punishment. Thus the glossator.

[THOMAS AQUINAS, *SUMMA THEOLOGIAE*]

It is to be seen in the doctor [Thomas Aquinas]:

By what means angels take on bodies in the first part [of the *Summa*],[88] and elsewhere. By what means those bodies obey as regards motion in space.[89] By what means they do not exercise the faculties of life.[90] By what means demons can perform wonders.[91]

On heresy,[92] idolatry,[93] and apostasy,[94] and by what means idolatry can be distinguished in kind and in type from heresy,[95] the second of the second part [of the *Summa*]. *Catholicon.* Heresy. Illusion.

Any man whatsoever can do anything whatsoever over a very long period [using] intelligence, diligence, science, or art according to human capacity; but the Devil can do the same thing—not in an instant, because there can be no motion in space in an instant, but in a very short time, imperceptible to us, and at great speed[96]—as regards the opening and blocking of ways, and the opening of whatever things are closed, by disjoining and rejoining, etc.

Demons can do everything that can visibly be done in this world, making use of physical objects, "by skillfully utilizing, through motion, the potential energies latent in nature";[97] they can also produce all kinds of movements of bodily objects very quickly. While these things may be achieved over a long time by various natural powers—which include the aforesaid latent energies—and [demons do this] by applying these powers to motion in space.

---

88. Cf. *ST* I, Q. 51, Art. 2.
89. Cf. *ST* I, Q. 53, Arts. 1–3.
90. Cf. *ST* I, Q. 51, Art. 3.
91. Cf. *ST* I, Q. 114, Art. 4.
92. Cf. *ST* II–II, Q. 11.
93. Cf. *ST* II–II, Q. 94.
94. Cf. *ST* II–II, Q.12.
95. Cf. *ST* II–II, Q. 94, Art. 1.

96. Cf. *ST* I, Q. 53, Art. 3.
97. This elegant translation of Aquinas's phrase is provided by Bernard Boedder in *Natural Theology* (New York: Benziger Bros., 1891), 431. Most of this paragraph appears to draw upon *ST* I, Q. 114, Art. 4.

With God's permission, demons are free to affect external matters via their practical intellect and will, for example, by applying their will so that movement results. And demons occupy a particular point in space as a result of an effective action, and thus they are located at whichever point where they have been active. And demons are executors of divine justice, and thus good angels also execute divine justice, albeit to another end.[98]

It is possible for demons to do many kinds of wonders involving the physical elements, as well as things consisting of the elements, which are movable objects [that may] move in a natural way, from or to a middle point, that is to say, up and down. Yet [demons] cannot be called creators because they act on preexisting matter created by God, and thus they depend upon the created matter and causality ordained by God as prime mover.

Physical bodies obey demons as regards motion in space by God's permission, and this applies to human bodies as well, especially when those men are willing participants.

---

98. Cf. *ST* I, Q. 114, Art. 1.

Invectives Against the Sect of Waldensians (Witches) (1460)

JOHANNES TINCTOR

Johannes Tinctor's *Sermo contra sectam Valdensium* appeared in Latin in 1460.[1] Within a few years, a French version of the text, probably translated by the author himself, was produced and disseminated in the Low Countries. The translation that follows is based primarily on Van Balberghe and Duval's 1999 edition of this Middle French text, clarified in a few places by the text of the Alberta manuscript (which we are editing separately).[2] We translated the Middle French text because it was the form in which this treatise had the widest circulation—in at least four deluxe manuscripts that ended up in noble and princely hands, and in a very early printed version (Colard Mansion, ca. 1476–84). Wherever the vernacular version strays from or omits parts of the original Latin, we include a translation of the relevant Latin passage. As in the *Recollectio*, we have used brackets to indicate subheadings that we inserted to help readers navigate

1. Scholars have referred to the French translation of Tinctor's *Sermo* in various ways; Franck Mercier, for instance, uses *Traité du crisme de vauderie,* while Jan Veenstra uses *Contre la Vauderie* (see Mercier, *Vauderie d'Arras,* 29; Veenstra, *"Fons d'aulcuns secrets,"* 437). For the sake of simplicity, we have followed the practice of the most recent editors and opted to use *Invectives contre la secte de vauderie,* the Middle French title attached to the treatise when it was printed by Colard Mansion sometime after 1475.

2. Jean Tinctor, *Invectives contre la secte de vauderie,* ed. Émile van Balberghe and Frédéric Duval (Tournai: Archives du Chapitre Cathédral, 1999). Among other things, Van Balberghe and Duval's edition includes a collection of critical notes providing references to dozens of scriptural and patristic sources. We have retained much of this (outstanding) scholarly work below, denoting references derived from this edition with the abbreviation VBD. We are also grateful for the contributions of several students in our demonology seminar in the fall 2013 and fall 2014 terms. Jeffrey S. Longard in particular provided numerous suggestions, revisions, and additions to these notes; we extend to him our most sincere thanks.

through parts of the text. These subheadings do not appear in the original manuscript.

[LIST OF CONTENTS]

The prologue of this work addresses the following topics:

- First the creation of the angels.
- *Item* the sin of the angels in general and of their punishment.
- *Item* the manner in which the angels sinned in particular.
- *Item* the pride of demons.
- *Item* that in the disposition of demons there are only two sins: namely, pride and envy.
- *Item* that demons are guilty of all the sins we do because they consent to them and are joyful if they are able to induce us [to sin] by tempting us.
- *Item* how the Devil tempted Adam.
- *Item* what the sin of Adam was.
- *Item* what the punishment was for the sin of Adam.

This treatise has two main parts.

- The first [part] addresses the grave evil of the crime of witchcraft,[3] and in order to demonstrate this, two principal sections will be introduced.
  - The first addresses the great crime in itself, and here in the first instance it is shown that the sin of witchcraft is worse than the idolatry of the pagans; and the causes that moved the ancients to idolatry are also explained.
    - *Item* shows how the sin of witchcraft is worse than the sin of heresy.
    - *Item* how the sin of witchcraft is worse than the sin of the wicked law of the Saracens [Muslims].

3. Literally, "Waldensianism"; here, actually, "witchcraft," using the older term for heresy to refer to this new crime.

- The second section addresses the disgrace and evils that would come from the continuation of this sect and shows, among other things, how if this sect continues to exist, it will cause the Antichrist to appear in this world.
- And then there are a number of calls for eradicating this sect, and first all people are exhorted in common, then the prelates, and finally the princes.

- The second part of this treatise speaks of the wonders that the Devil is said to do at the request of the witches [*vaudois*] and shows what he can in reality do, and what he can do only by illusion, and to this are added four teachings:
  - The first teaching regards the nature and method of the art of necromancy.
  - The second teaching concerns what demons accomplish in reality.
  - The third teaching speaks of the things that the Devil does by illusion and by mere appearance, without any reality, and shows by what means this is accomplished.
  - The fourth and last teaching is how one might discern and recognize when certain wondrous deeds are performed by the angels and when by demons.

[PROLOGUE]

"*Nevertheless through envy of the Devil came death into the world: and they that do hold of his side do find it.*"—This is the word of the Wise Man in the second book of Wisdom.[4]

GOD, ALL-POWERFUL CREATOR OF THE UNIVERSE, created all the spiritual beings of the heavens to be good and virtuous, giving them great gifts of nature and of grace, for, as Saint Augustine said,

---

4. Wisd. of Sol. 2:24 (VBD, 115). The Wisdom of Solomon (or Wisdom) is a second- or first-century B.C.E. sapiential book written in Greek, possibly by an Alexandrian Jew. It is con- sidered deuterocanonical by the Roman Catholic Church but apocryphal by Protestant churches, which is why it does not appear in Protestant Bibles.

with the noble nature that he gave them, he also endowed them with virtue and grace.[5] But as they had received from God at their very beginning free will that could change and tend to one side or the other and were not created in a state of unchangeable sanctity, some would acquire the crown of justice and of eternal glory by employing well these divine gifts. Some of these spirits, virtuously using these high gifts of God, received from the most just judge the banner of eternal beatitude, by which they were unchangeably confirmed in the glorious contemplation of the blessed Trinity, and were given eternal righteousness of will without ever being able to bend or deviate from it.

But the others, as though they did not recognize and disdained the high gifts they had received, arrogantly abused them and plotted evilly against the majesty of him who had given them these gifts. For the most noble Lucifer, who, at the beginning and as one might say, in the world's morning,[6] was born and rose up full of wisdom and perfect beauty, being in the midst of the delights of paradise, was covered and adorned by all the precious stones; and as holy scripture describes, his robe was covered with sardius, topaz, jasper, chrysolite, onyx, *brisils* [probably beryls], sapphires, carbuncles, and emeralds and was placed in the holy mountain of God to shine there and light the whole world with bright light.[7]

This most beautiful Lucifer, I say, so richly adorned, so generously endowed, blessed with such rich gifts, dared to exceed his place such that he presumed to ascend, as scripture says, to the highest heavens, and to erect his throne on the celestial stars. He wanted to make his seat in the holy mountain of the divine testament by rising above the height of all the clouds. And he went so very far in pride that he considered himself like the sovereign monarch.[8] But by the just judgment and correct vengeance of this monarch he was transformed

5. Augustine, *De civitate Dei* 12.9 (VBD, 115). *The City of God*, which explores the differences between spiritual and worldly ways of living and presents a specifically Christian understanding of history, is one of Augustine's most important and influential works. Book 12 considers, among other things, the nature of angelic beings.

6. Isa. 14:12.

7. Ezek. 28:13 (VBD, 115).

8. Isa. 14:13–14 (VBD, 115).

from the brightest and most adorned angel to the darkest and most detestable dragon; and from the heavens he fell to earth. He swept his tail after him and brought down a third of the stars, as scripture recounts.[9] So then, the high Creator, subjecting and laying low the proud and favoring the humble and the poor, left the arrogant and the rich abandoned and empty-handed.

In separating and pulling apart the light from the dark, he called the light "day" and the dark "night." Thus he illuminated those saintly and glorious spirits with his pure light, filling them with the radiant beauty of his eternal light, and made them into shining mirrors, without smudge or spot, in which the high divine majesty could be seen and known. But the other spirits gloried arrogantly in their own excellence, did not observe due measure, and were not content to remain in a state of well-ordered lordship. Once they relinquished their estate and limited powers, they were condemned by God's eternal decree. Therefore, they are forever bound in stocks, awaiting the great and last judgment. Thus all the proud and arrogant angels fell from the most lovely and most bright heavens to the earth of miserable darkness, covered in shadow and death, where there is no order to be found, but where all confusion and perpetual horror dwell. For as all the angels were created good, these twisted spirits, by their prideful, evil will, fell from the holy righteousness in which they were made.

Of the manner in which the angels sinned in particular

And it was impossible that they should in any other way have deviated from the path of this virtuous righteousness, for the winds of passion

9. The dragon falling from heaven to earth and sweeping down the stars is found in Rev. 12:4–9. This passage reflects the substance of several scriptural passages, including 2 Enoch 29:4–5, Isa. 14:12, and Rev. 12:4. However, the wording suggests that Tinctor's immediate source was Jude 6 and 2 Pet. 2:4. The story of Lucifer's fall is a conglomerate narrative based not only on these biblical passages but also on the early association in Enochic Judaism of Lucifer with Satan. The Latin name "Lucifer" was used from the third century onward by early Christians to refer to the leader of the rebellious angels in heaven.

or the prick of filthy habit could not occur to spiritual [angelic] beings in their state of righteousness. Thus their [the angels'] mind could not be bound by any ignorance or error that might have turned their will away from the real good. For the angelic mind could not choose real evil that appeared under the guise of the good. Thus it was necessary that a spiritual being's will should choose the real good corresponding to its nature; this will could not be perverted except by disdaining its proper order and the rule and measure which its sovereign had specified and granted. And in this disdain and transgression is the perversity of pride, for when the knowledge that one has of one's own excellence dominates and swells up one's courage to such an extent that one refuses and disdains to be subject to one's sovereign and does not deign to recognize that one has received that excellence from him, but in refusing to recognize his sovereignty and desiring, as it were, to exceed one's own measure, one desires to exceed the measure of one's own virtue.

Of the pride of demons

This evil angel, then, arrogantly wanted to be like God, for just as the Creator is by nature in a state of beatitude, the said Lucifer also wanted to add to his own power the dignity of eternal beatitude, presuming to attain it by his own and sole efforts, which, however, no creature can attain except by divine gift and grace. And he did not think to thank humbly the majesty of the Creator, or to render praise and thanks to him who is, as the Apostle says, all in all things, from whom, with whom, and in whom are all things.[10] And this proud ambition for distinction and excellence for himself made him immediately become envious of the advantages of humanity, for seeing the most excellent dignity to which man was by divine grace called to make up for and repair the effects of his fall, he [Lucifer] was wondrous sore

---

10. The first phrase is derived from
1 Cor. 15:28 (VBD, 115); the remainder of
the passage is derived from Rom. 11:36.

and envious. For what does it mean to be envious, other than to be pained over the advantages enjoyed by others, as one judges them to be somehow damaging or harmful to one's own good? Thus Aristotle says that a potter is envious of his neighbor potter,[11] for it seems to each one that the profit of his neighbor diminishes his own. For this reason, the proud are always battling one another and are never in agreement, for each one of them strives to attain high and surpassing glory, which is obscured and destroyed—or at least lessened—by company, for excellence desires utter singularity.

This most prideful spirit, then, felt himself seized by wondrous envy when he perceived himself to have been deprived and pushed out by righteous justice from the singular dignity that he had wanted with such a burning desire, and when he understood that man— which the hand of God had made and formed from the humus of the earth—had been called to that singular dignity and promoted [above him].

How there are in the disposition of demons only two sins: namely, pride and envy

Thus the entire perversion and malice of the disposition and will of demons lies in these two sins, that is, to wit, in pride and in envy, for it is impossible that sin should accrue within the desire for spiritual goods, if not by the two manners described above. And since the angel is by nature a spiritual being without any admixture of bodily substance, he cannot desire anything but spiritual goods. If his will leaves

---

11. Cf. Aristotle, *Rhetoric* 2.10. The reference to the potter's envy, as Van Balberghe and Duval note (155), also appears in Tertullian, *Ad nationes* 1.20. Tertullian (b. ca. 160 C.E.) was a prominent writer and apologist of the early Christian church. Book 1 of his *Ad nationes* (*To the Nations*), which addresses non-Christian peoples in the Roman Empire, challenges their false beliefs about Christians. It is ironic that Tinctor should invoke the same metaphor that Tertullian does, given that *Ad nationes* sets out to debunk Roman claims about activities, including infanticide, that were retained in the elaborated theory of diabolical witchcraft promulgated by Tinctor and his colleagues.

the correct path, it must be the result of pride and envy, as those sins are so much joined together and connected that the emotion of pride is inseparably and always accompanied by the emotion of envy, for the desire for any good and the rejection of its contrary issues from the same root. In the sense, then, that an individual desires and pursues without measure singular excellence out of pride, he also hates, on account of envy, the glory of others as taking away from his own. And even though it has been said that all the perversity of the [fallen] angels is contained in these two sins of pride and envy, it should not, however, be understood that the [fallen] angels are pure and innocent of all other vices, for, if they are not inclined to other sins beyond pride and envy—

How demons are guilty of all the sins we do because they consent to them and are joyful if they are able to induce us [to sin] by tempting us

—nonetheless they are guilty of all the others, and they should be called to account as they really consent to, and are guilty of, these other sins. For they take great pains and efforts to cause people to fall into these [sins] and work diligently to make them tumble into them, and they are prodded to do this incessantly by their astonishing envy, which makes them exult when they see people sinning and rejoice at their damnable deeds.

Thus this depraved spirit, casting off his Creator and abandoning himself to all evil, sinned quite soon after his creation and did not want to remain on the path of truth. He conceived, as it is said, an immense envy of the height and singular excellence of man, which he considered to have been elevated by divine gift above all corporeal creatures of the lower world and clearly to be lord over all beasts and other living things. He considered that man had been instituted by God, justly and righteously, and placed in the hand of his counsel [under God's advice], having free will and a full capacity to do that which would be pleasing to him [God].

How the Devil tempted Adam

And seeing him in the most delectable spot of the terrestrial paradise, [the Devil] approached him and made every effort and attempt to overthrow him. Then the Devil attacked him via temptations, and man was content to acquiesce to them.

What the sin of Adam was

And by that means he found himself thrown low, and as he believed the advice of the Devil, he also wanted, in his pride, to imitate him, for he desired, as his counselor had done, the appearance of divine majesty.

What the punishment was for the sin of Adam

The man, therefore, who—as long as he had remained on the path of righteousness on which he was first placed, would have been able to avoid spiritual and bodily death—at the instigation of the Devil his enemy, incurred certain death in both ways and delivered all his descendants to this obligation and bondage. Thus by the work of the Devil, death came into the world, and in this partake all those who are of his camp.[12]

The goal of the present treatise

And although this material which we have introduced concerns many difficult and lofty questions that would require a very long treatise if one wanted to get to the core of the matter as do the profound theologians who regularly work in this massive thicket, nonetheless we do not intend to deal with these subtle speculations, or to provide clever

12. Wisd. of Sol. 2:24.

students with material for exercises. Rather, we want to work with all speed to purge an ancient, vile, and corrupt yeast, full of all malice, and to uproot a horrible error which the common enemy, while people were sleeping, sowed and strewed in the midst of the good and pure evangelical wheat sown by Our Savior Jesus Christ;[13] and that is the most accursed and detestable sect which is called *vaudois* [witches], who, at the instigation of the most cruel and bloody enemy of humankind, has in these last days risen up and has now horribly infected a great part of Christendom, and has grown so much that it has even penetrated the farthest marches of France—which used to be free of such monstrous things and shone above all other countries in the purity of holy faith, and already—alas!—has deceived the souls of many to follow hateful errors and diabolical false illusions.

And certainly this horrible infection should be considered a miserable death, which has in these last days entered into the world by the envy of the Devil, whom those who are his allies—that is, those who are of this abominable sect—follow, and whom they adore and revere as the king and prince of all the proud, and to whom they make damnable sacrifices. In this miserable time, therefore, the god of the secular world [*princeps huius mundi*][14]—that is, the Devil—now blinds the thoughts of these pestilential people such that they see the truth of the true God as evil thoughts and lies and have chosen to serve and adore the creature instead of the Creator, who is praised and blessed forever and ever for all time.[15] And for this enormous sin, God has allowed them to forget all reticence to commit all vile and shameful things, and to bask in most abominable deeds, such as the horrific and execrable sins against nature, to name which seems to sully the mouth and defile and pollute the air. And if they receive by divine justice the recompense and wages due to their error,[16] they are most dishonorably destroyed and defiled with vilest filth.

---

13. Based on a conflation of 1 Cor. 5:7–8 and Matt. 13:24–25.

14. John 12:31 (also 14:30, 16:11). What follows is naturally conflated with a similar citation, 2 Cor. 4:4.

15. Rom. 1:25.

16. Perhaps an allusion to the latter part of Rom. 1:27.

The parts of this treatise

And because well-ordered brevity teaches and pleases more than endless words, I will force myself to keep my work within narrow limits, and I have conceived the intention to say mainly two things in this treatise.

THE FIRST PART

First of all I will work to expose the immense scope and most execrable malice of this crime in hating it, not as much as the seriousness of the offense would warrant, but as much as my modest capacities will allow, and to do this for the consolation of good and devout hearts, in order to defend them and preserve them for the sake of their salvation from these damnable deviltries.

THE SECOND PART

Second, I will declare the possible and likely means used by the subtle deceptions of the Devil to make and procure the things which are said to be done by the detestable members of this vile and most infamous sect; namely, whether the wonders they claim to have seen, heard, or performed are founded on any truth and if they occur in reality, or if they happen merely by illusion and deception of the imagination, the Devil thus maliciously abusing the thoughts of these same witches, such that they believe they actually see in reality what they see in their imagination, thinking they are real, being content with the images and appearances of things as though they were the real things themselves.

[PART I: ON THE DANGERS OF THE SECT]

How the sin of witchcraft is worse than the idolatry of the pagans

It is certain that this crime is entirely new and its like was never heard of, and I dare say that this sin of witchcraft is worse and more execrable than all the detestable errors of the pagans, which one finds to have existed from the beginning of the world right up to the present. I will prove this by two means: first, by the immensity of the crime in itself and by the wondrous abundance of its evil; second, by the most dangerous scandal which clearly comes from it, if it is not promptly suppressed.

Truly, this crime is of the greatest evil. It begins with apostasy and disdain for the Christian religion, for, as the Wise Man says, the beginning of all pride in man is turning away from God and estranging oneself from him by disdaining and condemning him.[17] If this apostasy, then, is the origin of pride, it also has to be the origin of all evil in general, for as the said Wise Man affirms, pride is the cause of all sin.[18]

Now, it is a well-known rule among the wise that the principles and origins of all things are more influential than all the rest, even though they are the lesser part in quantity. And just as in turning away from God there are varying degrees and different ways by which it can happen, this detestable sect of witches attains the first and highest degree. For just as all Christians have promised and solemnly sworn in holy baptism to believe, serve, and worship one God and Our Savior Jesus Christ, these unchristian and damnable witches have, with unbelievable temerity and audacious unbelief, forgotten it, despised it, condemned it, and abandoned it; and, moreover, with intolerable presumption, they defame, profane, and, as much as they are able, soil, stain, and pollute the most venerable and soul-saving sacraments of our Mother the Holy Church, and they even abuse, in their most abominable superstitions and most infamous and vile sacrifices, the most holy and divine sacrament of the altar, which is the precious remembrance of the holy passion and in which is contained all our redemption and salvation.

It would indeed be impossible to tell without dread in one's heart of how these most depraved practitioners of superstition come, in such a fraudulent manner, under the cover of hypocrisy and the pretense of being Christians, with the other, good Christians to Holy

17. Ecclus. 10:14. The book of Ecclesiasticus, or Sirach, is a Jewish wisdom book (ca. 200–175 B.C.E.) accepted as canonical by the Roman Catholic Church but regarded as apocryphal by Protestants.

18. Cf. Prov. 11:2, 16:18.

Communion on the days required by the church, and how, with a most wicked and filthy conscience and in the worst bad faith, they shamelessly present themselves to receive this most lofty and worthy sacrament. We have learned, by their own confession made in public court, about many of the most execrable crimes that they have perpetrated, both by abusing this divine sacrament and by other means. And a number of these horrible wicked crimes are recounted in the original Latin version of this treatise, but we shall refrain from putting each of them into French, lest any simple folks into whose hands this treatise should come might be led to their ruin by the incitement of the evil spirit [by reading such things].[19]

Let us therefore concentrate on the rest of the treatise, and let us agree that these damned and disloyal apostates, devoid of all shame, have abandoned the holy Christian faith and made of the depraved angel their god, and invoke his assistance in all matters, promising

19. The Latin text omitted here, printed by Van Balberghe and Duval (116), reads as follows: "Furthermore, [the sect], in its intolerable arrogance, desecrates and profanes the most holy and life-giving sacraments. Indeed, they abuse that most divine sacrament in which all of nature is restored, and is the vessel of redemption, for their own, most horrible, misguided, and superstitious goals. It is shameful even to say by what fraudulent means the practitioners of this superstitious cult come to Holy Communion under the pretense of Christianity, with most wicked consciences, on the days specified by the Church, along with others—faithful Christians. As appears in their confessions, [they do so] in order to pollute the most sacred host with their filthy mouths; and then [they] take it whole and spurn it, as they have been taught to do with the most sacred and life-giving mysteries by their leader. They then give it to filthy toads to eat, or at any rate to some other animals they have long tormented by starving them. Then, having taken blood from the bodies of innocent children whom they have treacherously killed, they make powders with the bodies of the toads, which they have reduced to ashes. Then they mix those ashes with the blood of the children to make an ointment, with which they anoint themselves according to the orders of their most accursed leader. And this (so they claim) renders them able to fly quickly through the air. And indeed, they misuse such powders superstitiously for all sorts of other nefarious acts—to destroy the crops, darken the air, cause earthquakes and thunder, and to do a thousand other pernicious acts contrary to the principles of brotherly [neighborly] love" (116; note to lines 324–25; fol. 203d in the Latin version). This corresponds exactly to the developing literary narrative of diabolical witchcraft that would soon be intensified and spread by the *Malleus Maleficarum* and that we know as the "elaborated theory" of witchcraft; see above, p. 7–10.

always to show him honor and reverence; and as scripture says, they make a pact with hell and an alliance with death.[20]

THE CAUSES THAT MOVED THE ANCIENTS TO IDOLATRY

Alas! Was there ever a more execrable, abominable, and detestable sect? Was not the idolatry of previous ages more pardonable because, as the book of Wisdom [of Solomon] recounts, men full of vanity, deprived of holy doctrine and knowledge of God, were unable to hear and could not recognize the Creator, and, not being careful enough of the things they saw, remained in ignorance of the sovereign worker from whom those things came?[21] If some thought that fire ruled the world and held it for God, others took the air to be God, others the wind, others the sea, others the stars, others the sun, and others the moon, sacrificing to them as if to the Lord and governor-general of the world.

And yet some others, more blind and plunging themselves into even deeper error, held the works of the hands of man to be God, such as gold or silver cunningly crafted, or images of beasts or some useless stone shaped and cut by some ancient craftsman. And similarly, when some woodworker, having felled a very straight-grained tree in the forest, carefully peeled off the bark and, working according to his craft, he made of it a fine lance or some other kind of staff to defend himself and protect his life; and from the rest of this wood made some nice dishes or a useful platter to serve his food on; [and] in the other wood, curved and knotty and useless, he roughed out a shape and in a hollow spot and by his ingenious art imparted to the wood the face and appearance of a man or an animal, anointing it with vermilion and giving it a color similar to that of a human being; and by painting it covered over all the spots that were previously to be seen, and made a niche in the wall where he placed it and attached it with iron lest it fall, knowing that it could not help itself and that it was nothing but an image he had made himself; yet nonetheless he afterward gave this, his work, such honor that he assigned it his riches and enquired of it regarding his wife and his children, and for their good health and

20. Isa. 28:15 (VBD, 116).   21. Wisd. of Sol. 13:1 (VBD, 116).

condition he pledged himself to it, and this poor fool was not ashamed to speak to something without a soul. Thus in order to have good health he prayed to something that had none, he begged a dead thing to give him a good life, asked for help from something that could not help him, prayed that on the road he should be guided by something that could not move and never took to the road. And in doing these things he asked for comfort and assistance from something that was utterly useless.[22] But I am dwelling too much on this.

Certainly, all these types of people were trapped in most damnable error, which their vain folly had invented, and yet, in brief, the said error came to an end. But in any case, their sins were far more bearable than those of these new people, for the above-mentioned ancient idolaters were inclined to show divine honors to a created being, for a reason which might help somewhat to excuse them. For some were moved to do this by boundless love and overflowing affection that they had for their friends, as the Wise Man recounts of a father, who, in his grief for the son whom death had so early taken from him, made for his consolation an image of his son, and for love of him adored and cherished it so much that he wanted to worship it as God, making his god of the image of him who was dead to him as a man; thus serving and obeying his tender affection, he imposed on stones and wood the incommunicable name of the divine.[23] Some were attracted to this folly by the pleasure that man naturally takes in a perfect representation. Some rude and simple folk, seeing images so well made that they represented the person in a lifelike way, were led to believe that images of such excellence might have some divine nature. And others believed this of the singular beauty and high majesty of the divine works [e.g., heavenly bodies, natural phenomena], and these are more worthy of pardon, for, as they fixed the eye of their intellect on the wondrous grandeur of these same works, the sovereign maker of which was unknown to them, they were moved to great admiration and, not thinking deeply enough, were moved to render them divine honors.

---

22. This lengthy passage (beginning with "when some woodworker") is taken from the Wisd. of Sol. 13:11–19.

23. Wisd. of Sol. 14:15 (VBD, 116).

PARTICULAR DECLARATION OF HOW THE SIN OF
WITCHCRAFT IS WORSE THAN THE SIN OF IDOLATRY

But these traitorous witches which my pen is now pursuing were not
cast into this madness by blindness or shadowy ignorance, by the
frailness of human pleasures or by an excess of tender and sweet love,
but rather they jumped into it of their own will by a mad obstinacy in
error, seeing and knowing what they were doing, and rebelling against
the divine light of the holy faith. And they said to God in their heart,
as Job tells of this sort of people, "Leave and get away from us; we do
not want to have knowledge of your ways."[24]

These damned people, then, as they had seen the invisible mysteries of God by the light of the holy Catholic faith by which they were
once adorned, and had known the lofty power and eternal divinity of
the Creator—not merely via visible creatures as the pagans did, but
also through the holy prophets and the evangelical law and that of
Moses, and by the preaching of Our Savior Jesus Christ and of his
glorious apostles—these detestable people, I say, instructed in the
lofty secrets and holy mysteries of the blessed Creator by so many
means, even though they knew God, nonetheless have not glorified
him as God and have not given him thanks or praise, but they have
lapsed and departed from him in their thoughts, and their foolish
heart has clouded over in their breast.[25]

And by a just vengeance they are so abandoned and rebuked by
the high judge that they are not content merely to relinquish the
precious and most faithful commandments of God—which are confirmed for eternity and made in all truth, equity, and justice—but they
also have risen arrogantly against the sovereign Lord, and make their
conventicles and assemblies to conspire against the sovereignty of the
prince of the universe and to scheme against the sacred majesty of
God and Our Savior Jesus Christ, and in many ways harm him who
watches over the earth and makes it tremble as he wills.

And by the execrable evils which they invent in their abominable
laboratories, they provoke him to wrath, who by his high power
touches the mountains and brings forth fire and light, and they open
their sacrilegious mouths to damn the divine majesty, and with this

24. Job 21:14 (VBD, 116).   25. Rom. 1:21.

they do great honor to him who is the enemy of God, and who by presumptuous arrogance arises against the Creator. And they hold him for their god who greatly, as they well know, hates the salvation and glory of humankind; they sacrifice their sons and daughters to him and at the same time spill the blood of innocents to perfume their damned sacrifices, and wipe away from their forehead the holy sign of *tau* of which the Apocalypse speaks,[26] and boast of themselves as being marked with the sign and character of the beast[27]—that is, of the Devil of hell—such that they can more openly and in more places practice the most damned exercises of their superstitious sect and busy themselves with the abominable crimes of their infamous and most execrable belief. It is therefore clear enough that the crime of the witches is beyond all comparison more grave than the sin of idolatry by the pagans.

How the sin of witchcraft is worse than the sin of heresy

Now let us see if the princes and grand inventors of the well-known and great heresies, such as Arius, Manicheus [Mani], Pelagius, Faustus [Faust of Riez],[28] and the like attained the perversity of these unfortunate people, and if the damnable heresies that once perverted the entire region of Asia and invaded the West as well were comparable to this newly introduced and never-before-heard-of evil.

And it is certainly true that these heresiarchs, by a firm obstinacy, made errors contrary and repugnant to the true Catholic faith and published and spread them everywhere they could, doing their

---

26. See Rev. 7:3. The *tau* (or "t") representing the sign of the cross is imagined in the book of Revelation as marking the servants of God (or "the elect") on the forehead; it is elsewhere referred to as a "seal" or as the "name of the Father and the Son" (Rev. 14:1).

27. Rev. 13:16–17.

28. Cf. VBD, 116. Other than Mani, these are ancient heretics or fig-ures after whom heretical or theologically deviant movements were named, specifically Arianism and Pelagianism; Faustus was seen as the originator of semi-Pelagianism. Manicheism was a dualistic religion that competed with Christianity in late antiquity and was seen as especially dangerous. Arianism and Manicheism were Eastern in origin; Pelagius and Faustus were probably both born in Britain.

best to defend them, according to their abilities. But they were not as arrogant as these people [witches] have been, for the heretics did not mindlessly impugn a known truth and did not willingly reject it of their own accord but, moved by a holy devotion, wanted to taste and attain a level higher than they ought; and thinking too highly of their own knowledge, [they] dared presumptuously to search and inquire into the sovereign majesty, and were weighed down by the exalted nature of glory and damnably strayed from the path of truth, but they did not know at any rate that they erred as these people do.

The heretics arrogantly perverted the teachings of the holy evangelical faith, but not knowingly; whereas these people mindlessly condemn and despise the commandments of God, the sovereign commander. The heretics honor the Creator at least in words, even though their heart is far removed from him,[29] but this pestilential people renounces God by their deeds and by their words blaspheme him. The heretics do not think they hold any communication or acquaintance with demons and detestable spirits, but these people are in familiar and most intimate company and perpetual alliance with them. The heretics were led astray and seduced by stubbornness, but these people are moved to their sins and swept away by obstinate evil and a form of diabolical perversity.

How the sin of witchcraft is worse than the sin of the Mahometans [Muslims]

And then what will I say of the detestable sect of Mahometans of whom the originator and inventor was the most infamous Mahommet [i.e., Muhammad], who by a most mysterious judgment of God was permitted six hundred years ago [*sic*] to occupy most cruelly the very rich and powerful kingdoms of the Orient, such as Persia, Libya, Egypt, Arabia, and many others, and holds them, alas, subject to

---

29. An allusion to Isa. 29:13 and Mark 7:6.

eternal damnation? Truly, the folly of these Mahommetists is utterly vile and unworthy and ought better to be called a bestial failing rather than a human vice. But nonetheless, I dare to affirm that the contagious and pestilential venom of the witches is worse by far and more dangerous and full of the greatest madness.

For the sect of the Saracens despises the mystery of the divine incarnation and of the holy cross, and by the wicked fraud of their law, contained in the book they call *Alcoram* [the Qur'an], and the detestable errors that are in it, they pervert the holy scriptures of the New and Old Testaments which affirm that this sovereign gift of God was given for the redemption of humankind—but yet this sect keeps the truth of the cultivation and adoration of the divine and detests idols and does not sacrifice except to God, and not to any creature. But the witches, by a sacrilegious presumption, take and remove from the holy divinity and glorious humanity of Our Savior Jesus Christ the high honor of adoration that is due him and which they too are obligated to render by virtue of the sacred and solemn profession made in holy baptism, and render this reverence to the evil spirit, raising up above them the prince of sinners and placing, as scripture says, the Devil at their right hand.[30]

The Saracens, weighed down by the long shadow of error, do not reckon with the salvific benefits that divine power secretly accords to humankind under the mysterious cover of the venerable sacraments of the church, and value these holy sacraments not at all, as they know nothing of the divine power and have neither hope of the wages of righteousness nor knowledge of the honor reserved eternally for holy souls. But the witches despise all these precious sacraments on which they were raised and abuse them in most detestable ways. And even the most holy sacrament of the altar, in which the price of our salvation is signified and remembered and also really and in truth contained—they do not shrink away from touching it with their execrable hands and abuse it in the most detestable fashion.

30. Matt. 25:33 (VBD, 116). The source is not clear, but Tinctor might be attributing to the witches a perversion of Ps. 16:8 (KJV).

[Other notes on the excessive evils of witchcraft]

And truly the sin that the witches commit in touching the holy sacrament of the altar is by comparison worse and more horrifying than that which some people committed in the Old Testament by touching irreverently the holy things of the old law. And the former crime exceeds the latter to the extent that the sacrament of the altar, in which Our Savior Jesus Christ is truly contained, is of greater holiness than the sacraments and vessels of the Old Testament, which were nothing but a figuration of the holiness and spiritual grace of the new law. And yet those who thus despised [the holy objects] at the time of the law of Moses were speedily punished and promptly felt the fury of the great judge, just as Ozias was struck dead on the spot because he touched the holy ark,[31] or Balthazar, king of the Chaldeans,[32] who presumed with those of his retinue to drink wine from the gold and silver vessels consecrated and dedicated to the holy temple, thus praising and glorifying his gods of gold, silver, bronze, iron, wood, and stone, for which misdeed that same king was killed that same night and his kingdom transferred to the Medes.[33]

Similarly, the Jew who followed the command of the most impious king Antiochus to sacrifice publicly to idols in the sight of all the people was punished on the spot by the most noble prince of the law named Mathatie [Matityahu], who, enflamed by the good and pious regard in which he held the law of God, went forward and killed him on top of his sacrifice and destroyed the said idol as well.[34] Furthermore, the pagans, indulging themselves in all pleasures, allowed themselves all luxuries, yet they did not stain themselves with the most noisome and execrable vices forbidden by nature.

But the witches are so caked in the mud of vile thoughts and are so vilely polluted in all their deeds and are so thoroughly enflamed,

---

31. 2 Sam. 6:6–7. Uzzah, son of Abinadab, reached out a hand to steady the ark when David was transporting it to Jerusalem.

32. I.e., Belshazzar, "King of Babylon" (probably regent) when Babylon was conquered by the Persians under Darius in 539 B.C.E.; cf. Dan. 5.

33. Dan. 5:1–4 and 28–31 in particular.

34. 1 Macc. 2:23–25. Protestants regard 1 Maccabees, like Wisdom of Solomon and Ecclesiasticus, as apocryphal.

consumed, and corrupted by their detestable desires that there is no abominable filth or deed of the flesh that is not pleasing to them, such that they do not even shrink from having carnal intercourse with the Devil transformed into the guise of an animal, of which the human heart cannot think without abomination and horror; and decency barely allows one to speak of it.

Moreover, the nasty pagans, even though they do not know of the holy path of salvific justice—as they are robbed and deprived of the light of the Gospel by their demerits—nonetheless retain some moral decency and prohibit, punish, and exterminate all vices that injure the public good, such as parricide, murder, homicide, adultery, and similar sins by which human society is much damaged and disturbed.

But these envenomed people, this most cruel brood of vipers, praise and approve all the above-mentioned execrable evils and do them as much as they can, holding in greater esteem those who most horribly defile themselves in these evil and abominable deeds.[35] And even, in order to be more pleasing to their master, king and prince of all depraved evil, they voluntarily offer to perpetrate these crimes and are moved by no hope to acquire any desired advantage, or by any passion or motive of desire, wrath or hatred, but subject themselves to all evils merely to give pleasure to the Father of Darkness, as everyone knows he loves to gorge on such dainties, to cultivate such sacrifices, and to honor such homage, services, and tributes.

And thus they take pains to both storm down the gorgeous wheat of the countryside with fogs and to burn it and dry it out, and to try to destroy by lightning the most agreeable fertility and abundance of the vine; at other times they strive to kill horses, horned animals [cattle], sheep and goats, and similar livestock, which is the guarantee of people's wealth, or at least according to their abilities to visit upon them long wasting diseases; sometimes they are intent upon the death of children and old people, and sometimes they terrify towns and fields with sudden hailstorms and unexpected bolts of lightning; at the same time, they are at pains to bring pestilence to the world, destruction of nations, wars, and commotions. And in these and similar malefic crimes, they exercise all their cunning and turn away

---

35. May be alluding to Rom. 1:28–32.

from other activities, and there is no crime so horrific that they would fear to undertake it, as long as they think it could in any way serve their most damnable religion, by which they greatly wish to please the evil spirit.

And surely it is no wonder if this evil and bastard people plunge themselves into the gulf and abyss of ills. For as they have estranged themselves and alienated themselves from God in all things, and by irreverence and their stiff-necked will have broken the bonds of the good and sweet prison kept by the most merciful and kind judge, having also broken the sweet yoke of the most pure and immaculate law of God, by which souls are converted and spirits purified; as they have, I say, liberated themselves and placed themselves outside obedience to the sovereign prince in all matters, and in obstinate courage have said to themselves, "I will no longer obey," they must throw themselves into all crimes and abandon themselves to all sins, such that their depraved will, not governed by the brake of reason, is thrown down and falls to the most profound depths of evil.

The Wise Man describes well an apostate when he says he is a useless man and walks with an evil mouth, agrees with his eye but speaks with his finger, shuffles with his foot and in his depraved heart always plans evil and always sows discord.[36] For because reverence for God is extinguished in a bad heart by apostasy, nothing remains there that could in any way be helpful for salvation, and because the root of all justice has been torn out, it is necessary that all human emotions, both of the heart and of the body, are troubled, in confusion and in disarray, and such men lose their way; and it is also necessary that the heart and mouth utter evil thoughts and other filth that stains a person, such as homicide, adultery, fornication, theft, false witness, and blasphemy, and that a man's feet run to evil and hasten to shed human blood.[37]

The Wise Man once again describes in more detail in another passage the detestable and most wicked life of this apostate people, speaking in this way: "It is not enough for them," he says, "to be in error against the wisdom of God, but, living in the great war of ignorance and error, they call such great and horrible evils peace." And he

36. Prov. 6:12–14 (VBD, 117).   37. Isa. 59:7.

notes in particular the sins that they commit, saying: "They sacrifice their children to idols or perform other abominable sacrifices, their night vigils are full of madness, and they do not maintain their widowhood or marriage without some vile stain. Rather, either they kill one another out of envy or they bother and anger one another by adultery, and they mix together all the following things: blood shed by homicide, theft, fraud, corruption, disloyalty, trouble, perjury, a tumultuous confusion of the goods given by God, forgetting the souls of the dead, defiling of birth, inconstancy in marriage, disordered and very unruly luxury."[38] The worship of detestable idols is, clearly, the cause, beginning, and end of all evil, for the idolaters either rave madly in their joyous festivals or spew forth evil tales to injure others, or live unjustly, or perjure themselves without a thought.

Indeed, if one considers the deeds of the infamous witches, one will clearly see that they do all these things listed above and that they imitate and follow the evil spirit in his manifest deeds so diligently that they are the most intimate and principal servants of the Devil, by whose envy death came into the world.

And truly the Devil is well named Behemoth by Job, of which our Lord spoke to Job from out of the whirlwind, as scripture describes,[39] and told him that his force is in his loins and his power in his navel.[40] This ancient serpent called Behemoth sleeps, says scripture, in the secret quiet of the reeds,[41] that is to say, in thought deceived and led astray by vain superstition, which is empty and devoid of grace and justice, like a reed; and it rests in the moist places of hearts filled with and swimming in the fog of carnal filth, and the shade of the reeds hides and protects his shadow, that is to say, that the multiplicity and infinity of the evils of these witches intensify somewhat and redouble the stubborn evil of the Devil, who leads them to perdition; and the green willows of the stream paddle them, that is to say, that the mad people, planted and collected at the stream of all delights, sprinkled with the sweet water of the holy Catholic faith, are content to acquiesce

---

38. May be alluding to Wisd. of Sol. 14:22–28 (VBD, 117).

39. Job 40:15–24. Behemoth is a primeval chaos monster of the land, usually imagined as a vast land animal,

and a parallel to the maritime chaos monster Leviathan. Tinctor associates Behemoth with the Christian devil.

40. Job 40:16 (VBD, 117).

41. Or willows. Job 40:22.

and to obey his detestable commands and most depraved exhortations and hasten to gratify as much as they can his ill will, as they are always dressed and ready to do so.

The said Behemoth will swallow up the river, that is, this unstable and fickle people, and it will not be reckoned of him, for it is his usual prey and he has confidence that the River Jordan must flow down and into his mouth,[42] that is to say, he hopes to devour the rest of Christendom via a similar or other temptation and to draw them into hell with the most accursed witches.

It is certain that any period would be too brief, and my ability to speak would be destroyed, if I wanted to say as much about this as the matter requires. Therefore, having regard to the time available and to my own comfort, I will of my own volition stop enlarging and expanding in this way and will put an end to this first section, recapping what has been said in the different parts.

Summary of the first section

Whoever considers the development of this argument will clearly recognize that the sect of witches is the worst and the most abundant and overflowing in evil of any that have ever been discussed, for it distances itself even further from the Creator, entering more deeply into the region of dissimilarity, as scripture says,[43] and makes a more intimate alliance with the Prince of Darkness, by which it more greatly shows its disdain for God and the holy sacraments and insults them more [than any other sect]. Furthermore, it busies itself with more sorts of crimes and commits and glories in more horrible and abominable crimes. Thus it clearly appears that there is no worse evil than that of the witches, and that it surpasses, as the theologians say, all

---

42. Job 40:23.

43. The phrase "the region of dissimilarity" in fact appears in Augustine's *Confessions* 7.10 (VBD, 117). The *Confessions*, Augustine's spiritual autobiography, is one of his most influential works; chapter 10 of book 7 reflects on the merits of searching for divine guidance by withdrawing into one's "inward self." See http://www.newadvent.org/fathers/110107.htm.

others in intensity and extent. And here ends the first section [of the first part].

The second section addresses the scandal of evils that would occur from the continued existence of this sect of witchcraft and shows among other things that if this sect continued, the Antichrist would come into the world on account of it

The second section also serves to show that which is said, taken from the immense scandal that the Devil is able to make by this sect—the Devil, adversary of human salvation, who, like a roaring lion, is always looking to see whom he can devour[44] and eternally swallow up. And this section takes as its argument the question, if the heretic Arius, who was nothing but a single spark in Alexandria, made the flame of his error fly through the whole world, as Saint Jerome says,[45] and burned almost all of Christendom with the fire of heresy, because it was not immediately extinguished and smothered, what should one then think of this most harsh and poisonous fire of witchcraft? Which burning torches of malice will light holy Christendom if this eternal fire and the infernal madness of this fire are not extinguished by the living water of salvific wisdom, and if the fire is not truly exterminated and annihilated by the sharp sword of the word of the Gospel and the bitter scourge of vengeance and rigorous judgment?

If this is not done, false prophets, as scripture says, will shamelessly take on the flesh of pestilence and pervert the principles of holy scripture, and will interpret inconvenient testimonies to suit themselves.[46] And in bold confidence, [they] will say all the evil things in the world, against the truth, and will give people the secret and dishonest waters of evil heresy, which will seem good to some because they are novel. And [they] will also offer openly and with impunity

44. 1 Pet. 5:8.

45. Jerome, *Commentarius in epistolam S. Pauli ad Galatas* (*Commentary on Paul's Letter to the Galatians*), 3.430 (VBD, 117). One of the doctors of the early church, Jerome (ca. 347–420)

translated the Bible into Latin and produced a sizable body of historical works and commentaries. The commentary on Galatians, to which Tinctor refers, was penned circa 387 C.E.

46. 2 Pet. 2:1 (VBD, 117).

the secret bread of schismatic rebellion, which some will, in like manner, judge more sweet than the ordinary bread of holy obedience. They
will provide complete and easy entry into all errors and will encourage
boldly all crimes and malefices because, as scripture says, they will
wet down and anoint the wall without a proper mixture and will sew
pillows beneath the heads of those who listen, appealing to their
desires, telling them agreeable vanities, and prophesying nonsense
and lies[47] they know will be pleasing to them. No one will be prohibited from going to the assembly of the evil and following their advice.
Everyone will have the freedom to remain in the path of sinners and
to make assemblies against God and Our Savior Jesus Christ. The
synagogue of Satan[48] will be wide open and the church of saints
closed.

And in this assembly the beast with seven heads and ten horns
will preside, as the Apocalypse says.[49] It will open its mouth to blaspheme God and make war on the saints and will conquer and overcome them, and will have power over all nations, peoples, and races
of all languages. And all the inhabitants of the earth whose names are
not inscribed in the book of life of the holy lamb, killed since the
creation of the world, will worship it—that is to say that this immaculate lamb was predetermined to die ever since the beginning of the
world in order to redeem humankind. Truly, there will then be no
discipline of behavior, observance of laws, order of justice, humanity
of life, protection or defense of the public good, or fear and reverence
of God. All will be in confusion and disarray. Each depraved and each
evil person shall live exactly as he pleases; the evil will usurp lordship
and government, and the holy and humble people will wail and beg
in desolation.

And indeed, just as the King of Darkness is delighted to hear lies,
he will have nothing but depraved servants as companions. Then wars,
murders, disputes, seditions will ravage kingdoms, cities, and fields.

---

47. A rather confused rendering of
Ezek. 13:18.
48. The phrase comes from Rev.
3:9.
49. This passage is from Rev. 13:1,
6–8. The beast of the book of Revelation was associated in late antique and
medieval Christianity with "the Antichrist," another figure based on a few
biblical references and constructed as a
coherent figure in the form of an apocalyptic adversary to Christ.

People will kill one another and bring death upon one another. Friends and neighbors will harm one another, children will rise against the old and the wise, and peasants will attack nobles: one will see in the cities nothing but execrable evil, rebellions, and defiance. Day and night, iniquity and evil will haunt the walls of towns and cities, anguished pain and unjust servitude will be always in the midst of cities, and there will never be any lack of usury or fraud. People will shamelessly rape virgins, pollute themselves with their next of kin, and commit detestable adultery, and all will be marked by most execrable luxury; everywhere public brothels will be built and, as scripture says,[50] at the head of each road and at the end there will be some sign of baseness, and there will be fornication so horrible that the like was never heard.

And the abominable iniquity of Sodom will seem righteous compared to this filth, for, as scripture says, the sin of Sodom was pride, excessive abundance of bread and all goods and getting drunk and eating beyond measure, her idleness and her daughters' [idleness], and they did not take care of the needs of the poor and suffering nor stretch out their hand to aid and comfort them.[51] And truly all the sins recounted here are lesser and more bearable than the most execrable crimes to which this accursed people of witches give themselves over.

It is certain, then, that the generations of whom the Wise Man speaks in Proverbs will rise up, saying that they do things much to be feared, and it is the generation that curses their father, that is, their Celestial Father, and that does not wish to bless its mother,[52] that is to say, the church, which by the holy washing of spiritual rebirth brings forth children by adoption; [it is] also the generation that judges itself to be pure and clean, while it affirms that evil is good and that the darkness is light.[53] And nonetheless, as this Wise Man says, this generation's feet are not washed, that is to say that their affections and desires are stained with all sorts of abominable filth.

---

50. Ezek. 21:24 in the Vulgate; the KJV appears not to retain this reference in its translation of Ezekiel.

51. Ezek. 16:49.

52. Prov. 30:11 (VBD, 118).

53. Prov. 30:12 (VBD, 118). The allusion to Proverbs is there, and Tinc-

tor seems to continue his list of citations from the same passage (see the two following), but the direct citation is from Isa. 5:20.

And the generation will rise up, as the Wise Man says, whose eyes are lifted up and their eyelids are on high,[54] by which we understand that this generation is exceedingly proud, and, lacking all sobriety of spirit, feels and enjoys haughtiness. And in all arrogance, as the same one says, will rise up a generation with rough teeth used as swords, and which has sharpened its jaws to eat the famished and devour the poor.[55]

And with this accursed generation will appear the formidable host of evil people whom the Apostle has predicted will reign in the last days, and those who will relinquish the faith and will believe deceitful spirits and the teaching of demons, speaking lies and hypocrisy, and those who will have their consciences pierced by malice.[56] There will also come most dangerous times when people will love themselves beyond measure, lovers of money, boastful, arrogant, blasphemers, disobedient to their parents, ungrateful and most unholy, also people without love and good affection and without peace, cursing, self-indulgent, cruel, rebellious, swollen with conceit, loving pleasure more than God and who pretend to be godly, denying the power of godliness and who do not recognize truth.[57]

And some of these people, as the Apostle says, enter houses and captivate simple women who are overwhelmed by their sins and are made prisoners of the Devil, [and] who are led by many and useless desires, always wanting to learn though they never arrive at knowledge of the truth[58]—and this contains some of the disasters that will certainly happen, if this depraved sect is suffered to continue and is not exterminated.

But all this is nothing in comparison with the other evils that will certainly come to pass if this cruel and evil pestilence continues to afflict and disorder the world as it has begun to do. It is probable that the most perilous time of which the prophet Daniel once spoke will come, saying that when iniquities and injustice have reached full measure, a king will rise up with a bold countenance and without any shame.[59] He will invent new doctrines and square the propositions of the holy faith according to his own understanding. And the power of

54. Prov. 30:13 (VBD, 118).
55. Prov. 30:14 (VBD, 118).
56. 1 Tim. 4:1–2 (VBD, 118).
57. 2 Tim. 3:1–5.

58. Mainly from 2 Tim. 3:6–7 (VBD, 118); Tinctor has added "prisoners of the Devil."
59. Dan. 8:23 (VBD, 118).

this king will be confirmed and full, but not of his own doing. He will put all to waste and desolation, far beyond what one might be able to believe, and he will prosper in his accursed works and do as he pleases. He will kill the strongest and most valiant and will kill the holy people as he likes. He shall make deceit prosper in his own hand and he will glorify and magnify himself in his heart in all arrogance; he will have abundance of worldly goods and will kill huge numbers of people. He will rise up against the prince of princes and at the end he will be vanquished, broken, and extinguished, but not by human hands, as this will be done by the high and invisible power of the sovereign prince.[60]

By this proud king we should understand the Antichrist,[61] the son of perdition, who Saint Paul the Apostle predicted would be revealed and known at the end of ages.[62] And, as the said Apostle recounts, our Lord Jesus Christ will kill this Antichrist by the breath of his mouth and will destroy him by the light and brilliance of his glorious coming. And as the Apostle says, the coming of the Antichrist will be by the hand of Satan, and there will be nothing but deception and lies in all his signs, and all the wonders that he does will serve to seduce and evilly entrap people and make them die and lead them to damnation; and many evil people will allow themselves to be seduced and perverted by him, for they will not have wanted to receive the pure light to save themselves.

It is clear, therefore, from the foregoing, that whoever reads holy scripture diligently will see clearly that there is no crime or sin in the world that one might expect mortal men to avoid. So many dreadful dangers, as has already been demonstrated, would be brought by this execrable superstition of witchcraft if it should expand and grow. For if what we have already said is true—and certainly yes, it is without a doubt true, as it all comes from the holy scriptures which cannot lie

---

60. Dan. 8:24–25.

61. 1 John 2:18. The "Antichrist" and "Antichrists" in 1 John and elsewhere became, in later antique Christianity, a single figure equated with Revelation's beast, a kind of counterpart to Christ who would appear at the end of days to oppress and lead the righteous astray, fight the forces of good, and finally perish in battle, leading to the second coming of Christ.

62. The remainder of this passage is based on Paul's warnings in 2 Thess. 2:1–12 regarding a "man of sin" whose arrival will mark "the day of Christ" (i.e., the end times) (cf. VBD, 118).

or tell untruths—thus, since nothing could be more true, if this sect of witchcraft were to grow more and more and to grow as it has started, it would introduce and cause in a brief time the vast and astonishing tribulation of which there has been no equal since the world began and the like of which will not be found until the end. This tribulation, as scripture says, will be so harsh and cruel that no mortal person might survive it if the days of this most dreadful tempest were not cut short by divine mercy.[63]

Summary of this second and last section

If, then, it is to be believed, as I said, that the continuation and the growth of this cursed and infernal sect of witchcraft will bring the last tribulation with the Antichrist, it is certain that of all the detestable evils of this world, this is the most execrable, the most terrifying, and the one that ought most to be avoided, persecuted, and eradicated. And here we shall end the second section, which proposed and showed and confirmed all this.

Exhortation to all and sundry

And since it is as I have said, I hope that the desire for good and holy zeal for Christianity will now rise up against these mad people, and that the entire world will go to war with them in earnest. I hope that each and every one will distance himself from the detestable lairs of this evil and most damnable people, so that he will not be caught up with them and seem to be one of them, and that each and every one will apply all his mind, efforts, and ability to repulse and wipe out this most horrible evil; and as much as he can, let each person work in his calling to extinguish these evildoers; and as scripture commands, not to suffer them to live peacefully in their most abominable evil.[64]

63. Matt. 24:21–22 (VBD, 118).   64. Cf. Exod. 22:18.

Exhortation to the prelates

To you, your Graces, prelates of the church and doctors of scripture, I now address this discourse. Wake up, for the sake of God, and hasten to purge the vile, diseased, and corrupt yeast of this error,[65] engrained in the polluted hearts of the abominable witches. Cry out without ceasing and raise your voices against these most accursed inventions. Make public with all diligence the most execrable crimes of this most damnable sect. Sound the trumpet of holy doctrine and the silvered clarion of evangelical preaching, and warn the people to beware of the poisoned sword of this accursed people. Go up chivalrously on the wall to protect the fortress of the true Catholic faith. Be the bulwark and shield of the house of Israel, that is, of holy Christendom.

You now have a wonderful opportunity to make oral confession in public, for the salvation of all, of that which you believe in your heart to be your personal justification. And if you do it otherwise—and let it not be so—you will not have discharged the duties of your high and worthy office, and will be counted among the fainthearted and disloyal dispensers of the holy mysteries of God. You would truly be useless as shepherds of the flock of the sovereign pastor Jesus Christ, just as dogs who are silent at the sight of wolves and cannot bark at all are abandoned as useless by good and diligent shepherds. Certainly, at a time of such great adversity and such hard temptation, if you hide the wheat the Lord has given you to distribute in case of need, you will be cursed by all the people.

For the sake of God, remember how the holy martyrs went about the entire world covered in rough goatskins and most austere clothing, and how they were always in a state of suffering and anguish, sorely afflicted. Remember that these holy martyrs suffered much shame and villainous mistreatment, and beyond this, they were often harshly bound in prison. Recall to your memory how some of them were stoned, some had their bodies cut up with saws, some were hacked to death [by broadswords], and others were pierced by

---

65. An allusion to 1 Cor. 5:7–8.

[pointed] swords.[66] And yet, in the midst of all these harsh persecutions and horrible torments, they spoke openly in the presence of impious kings and most cruel tyrants, and constantly spoke what the Holy Spirit taught them to say, and were not hindered, no matter how they were frightened, from constantly and without fear preaching the holy doctrine of the Gospel; and they brought more people to Jesus Christ by their death than they did in their lifetime. And the Christian faith was not even very popular among the people at that time. And so, your Graces, how might you have security of the heart and repose of conscience if you are silent now, when the study of evangelical doctrine and good devotion flourish on earth? How, I say, would you dare to be silent, seeing the wondrous dangers and these terrible perils and attacks on the Christian religion, and equally among yourselves, who have such abundant riches and luxuries, and who have such resources to diligently discharge your duty to safeguard the holy Catholic faith and the salvation of the souls which God has given into your care?

Truly, in this case, your dissimulation would be most sinful and a grave fault, and it would certainly nourish and sustain that disloyal miscreancy, if you were to become companions in their sins. By keeping silent and by dissimulating you would, as scripture says, put your part and portion with these evil adulterers and most execrable sinners.[67] For, as Saint Gregory says, just as many people are led into error by foolish and ill-advised talk, so also many persevere and stay in their error due to undiscerning silence.[68] The holy zeal of God will then inflame and devour you, as scripture says,[69] and will make you speak good and virtuous words in defense of the faith. You will present your tongue humbly, as scripture says, to be the worthy pen of the very rapid writer who writes so easily,[70] that is, the sovereign master, the glorious and blessed Holy Spirit. You will do your duty, I hope, to

66. The paragraph to this point alludes to Heb. 11:35–38.

67. Ps. 50:18 (KJV) (Ps. 49:18 in the Vulgate; VBD, 118).

68. Gregory the Great, *Liber regulae pastoralis* (*The Book of the Pastoral Rule*, or *Pastoral Care*) 2.4 (cf. VBD, 118). Gregory's treatise, written circa 590 C.E., reflects on the ethical and behavioral standards expected of bishops and considers their duties to their flocks. It is thus appropriate that Tinctor cites the text in the context of an appeal to prelates.

69. Ps. 69:9 (KJV).

70. Ps. 45:1 (KJV).

prepare your courage to meet this high goal, and our Lord will govern and lead your tongue.

You[71] will put on the holy armor of God[72] and you will equip yourselves with his weapons, so that you can resist these sharp needles and harsh attacks of the Devil. You do not need now to take the field and fight against corporeal enemies of flesh and blood like yourselves, but you must wage war on the governors of this darkness and of the present age, which are the demons. You must do battle with the spiritual evils[73] that fell from the heavens long ago, and you must take the superb and shining armor that the Holy Spirit has made for you, his champions, and which you put into the best shape with all due care, so that you can [continue to] withstand the heavy load of that great and terrible day on which all evil was spread out over the earth. Provide therefore for your needs to that point that you lack nothing required for so cruel and fearsome a war. Clothe yourselves in the steeled hauberk of holy justice, gird your loins with constant truthfulness, don your boots in all haste and prepare your feet to go virtuously to all places to preach the holy Gospel of peace. Take the strong shield of true faith with which you will be able to extinguish all the burning and flaming darts of the most depraved and rebellious enemy. Take also the holy helmet of eternal salvation and the spiritual sword of the word of God. Arm yourselves with holy praises and devout prayer. Ask constantly for God's help and without ceasing pray to him with a fervent spirit for his assistance. And please diligently beg the sovereign master that it please him to preserve all good and saintly persons from these horrible evils.

---

71. From here to the end of the section, Tinctor bases his appeal directly on Eph. 6:11–18.

72. Here, the Latin diverges from the Middle French translation: "And on account of that, you will put on the armor of God so that you will be able to resist evil on that day, and to stand against all, garbed perfectly in the breastplate of justice, your loins girded in truth and your feet shod in order to prepare the way of the gospel of peace" (fol. 207d in Gerson, *Opuscula*; cf. VBD, 118).

73. Here, the various French translations of the text present interesting variations on the Latin original: the Brussels, Oxford, and Mansion copies render this word "milices" (hosts or armies), while the Paris and Alberta manuscripts opt for "malices" (evils).

Exhortation to the princes

Now it is time for me to address myself to you, most noble and most excellent princes, who are called by the sovereign prince to judge iniquities and condemn evildoers. Do your utmost for the love and reverence of God, and valiantly defend the cause of your Creator. Shake off and with all your might break the detestable bonds of evil of these rebellious witches. Throw far away their most envenomed yoke. You have been established by God as the cutters and harvesters of his fine field of wheat, and now comes the harvest season. Rip out, then, and gather this nasty weed and most stinking cruelty and bind it into sheaves to set on fire, and assemble in the barn the good and pure wheat,[74] thus giving peace to the loyal Christians and perfect rest to true Catholics.

For God's sake, remember that you do not carry the sword without a reason. Indeed, by this you are given to understand that you are ministers and officers of God charged with meting out strict justice to those who do ill and punishing delinquents decisively.[75] Thus your just sword will punish and will fall furiously upon these most cruel enemies of the Christian religion. You will persecute without quarter this poisonous and pestilent people, and by this you will make good Catholics flourish in sweet and secure peace while terrifying all evildoers.

It is written on this topic that because sentence is not passed on evildoers quickly, they commit their crimes without any caution or fear, and the fool often leaves his folly and becomes wise, if he often sees harsh punishment meted out to sinners and criminals. However, regardless of any of this, my intention is not to work to see criminal justice done, for it is all in all repugnant and contrary to my calling, for I am called to the holy priesthood and the sacerdotal estate, a humble servant and minister of the sovereign and eternal priest, who, as he says by the mouth of the prophet, does not desire the death of the sinner.[76] But I am bold enough to admonish, in all charity and sincerity, all princes and judges, and I want to move them, so far as I am able, to

74. Alluding to Matt. 13:30.   76. Ezek. 18:23.
75. Alluding to Rom. 13:4.

acquit themselves of the duties imposed on them by the high judge, that is, that in fulfilling the needs and responsibilities of their offices, they see to the peace and salvation of their subjects, and that, if there is need for the sake of the common good among the multitude, they are content to abandon to temporal destruction those whom they find guilty of these most execrable crimes. For, as Saint Jerome says, we must slice and cut off from a human body rotten and diseased flesh in order to ensure that the rest of the body is not corrupted and ruined. We must also turn out of the common stable the diseased sheep to preserve the healthy flock from infection and disease.[77]

And Saint Augustine corrected his statement according to which no one must be forced to preserve the unity of Jesus Christ.[78] He said that his statement was not overcome and vanquished by those who objected to it, but by the examples set and the deeds done by those who worked differently. For the fear of the law, as he says, produces such great riches for some; and it was very profitable and useful that many praised and thanked our Lord, saying, "Grace and praise to him who shook and broke the bonds by which we were held."[79] And thus Saint Augustine said, "There is not one of us who wants any heretic to die and be damned, but the house of David would not have been able to obtain peace had his son Absalom not died in the war he led against his father."[80]

Thus the holy and Catholic Church feels a mighty pain in its heart when it is constrained to send to damnation some of its children in order to save the others, and even though this damnation is for the good, salvation, and deliverance of all people, it cannot condemn

77. Jerome, *Commentarius in epistolam S. Pauli ad Galatas* 3.430 (VBD, 118).

78. Augustine, *Epistula* 93, 5.17 (VBD, 118). As bishop of Hippo (North Africa), Augustine played a pivotal role in crushing the heresy of Donatism (after Donatus), according to which priests who had betrayed Christianity under Roman persecution or had been ordained by such a priest were unable to perform the sacraments properly. Invoking Augustine in a context like this one is usually meant to justify the use of force against one's opponents on the grounds that they are in moral error. (Augustine's Letter 93 [408 C.E.] argues among other things that worshippers who have fallen into error may be compelled into orthodoxy. See http://www.newadvent.org/fathers/1102093.htm.)

79. Aquinas, *ST* II–II, Q. 10, Art. 8.

80. Augustine, *Epistula* 185, 8.32 (VBD, 118). For the full text of Augustine's Letter 185, see http://www.newadvent.org/fathers/1102185.htm.

people without its tender and maternal heart moaning in pain. Indeed, most noble princes, it is clearer than the light of noon that nothing more salutary can happen to you, nor can you earn greater praise, than if you have a most ardent zeal to safeguard and preserve the solemn institutions of God and of his holy church. For you are charged with the defense of the Christian commonwealth and can have no more glorious and honorable occupation in this world than to give yourselves over in all diligence to the punishment and extermination of those who commit such execrable crimes. It is certainly your business to not allow offenders against divine law to live in peace and to put their evil will into action, but you should, according to need and their case, punish them.

Truly, you are obligated to take just vengeance for the crimes they have committed against divine majesty, and you should equally defend and preserve all good people, and purge the church of the abominable and intolerable filth of these horrible sinners. Oh, most excellent princes, remember the glorious past. May it please you to recall to your mind's eye the lofty exploits and memorable deeds that the most noble princes did long ago out of the ardent devotion they had for the holy law of God. May it please you, for God's sake, to imitate and follow them, now that you have such a fine opportunity to do so. In doing so, you will earn sovereign celestial glory, and the praise of the world, which will last forever for you and your descendants. Gain for your name perpetual blessings from the mouths of the people. Look here and consider carefully how many fine examples and shining mirrors holy scripture offers you.

Was not the holy patriarch Abraham proved firm, constant, and loyal in the face of the temptations that assailed him? Indeed, this redounded to his credit and was ascribed to him, as scripture says, for perpetual righteousness.[81]

Did not the good Joseph, at the time of a terrifying famine, keep inviolable the holy commandments of God? For that reason he was promoted to lordship over the entire land of Egypt.[82]

---

81. 1 Macc. 2:52 (VBD, 118); also Rom. 4:3.

82. Gen. 39–41.

Pinchas,[83] from the depth of his devotion and holy zeal for the faith of God, executed the Jew who was publicly transgressing the commandments of the law, and by this he merited the witness of the holy and eternal priesthood.[84]

Jesus, guaranteed by fulfilling the word and commandment of God, was elected to have government over the people of Israel and to be their duke and principal leader.[85]

Caleph [Caleb] obtained a fine inheritance in the Promised Land by openly and loyally witnessing before the entire assembly and church of the Jews.[86]

David, in the great mercy he always practiced, came to be king of all Judah, and the throne of his kingdom will last forever in the person of Our Savior Jesus Christ, who is his descendant.[87]

Elijah the prophet was carried off alive to the terrestrial paradise because he pursued the law of God with such great ardor and courage.[88]

The three children named Ananie, Azaie, and Misael,[89] whom the tyrant Nebuchadnezzar had thrown into the furnace, were delivered

83. That is, Phinehas, priest during the Israelites' exodus from Egypt. Because of his violent zeal to punish and stop "idolatry" and immorality, he is proposed here as a model of diligent lay justice.

84. Num. 25:7–13.

85. Van Balberghe and Duval reject the reading "Jesus nane par ce," as they see no possible function for "nane." We have read it as a version of *nan, nant,* guarantee, pledge, deposit, though their reading makes as much sense.

86. Num. 13–14; Josh. 14:6–14. Caleb urged the children of Israel to go forward into the Promised Land and take it.

87. Luke 1:32–33.

88. Tinctor might have confused God's "taking" Enoch (Gen. 5:18–24, glossed in Heb. 11:5 as meaning that Enoch's body was never found, and thus that God had physically taken him while alive) with the ascent of

Elijah, in 2 Kings 2:11–12, being carried up by a flaming chariot. Conversely, the Elijah story might be considered sufficient for Tinctor's version: Elijah was caught up alive from earth to heaven. Cf. 2 Kings 2:1 ("Now when the LORD was about to take Elijah up to heaven by a whirlwind") and 2:11 ("a chariot of fire and horses of fire separated the two of them, and Elijah ascended in a whirlwind into heaven") (NRSV).

89. The Hebrew forms Hananiah, Misha'el, and Azariah (in the order of the biblical text) of the better-known Chaldean names Shadrach, Meshach, and Abednego (Dan. 1:7), referring to the three Israelites devoted to God whom Nebuchadnezzar had thrown into a fiery furnace for not bowing down to a great idol; they were saved by divine intervention. The three men first appear in Dan. 1:6; the story of the furnace is in Dan. 3.

by divine intervention from the flames on account of the constancy of their faith.

Daniel the young prophet, by virtue of his just simplicity and benign gentleness, was saved from the savagery of the lions.[90]

I will refrain from mentioning the glorious and victorious martyrs of the new law, for there is no need for me to illuminate them or make them known. They are certainly known well enough by each and every Christian by the worthy commemoration and festivals by which the church each year celebrates them, recalling the lofty triumphs and the highly regarded victories they won by their burning love of the holy faith of God. Nor will I speak here of the holy doctors or of their glorious deeds in defense of the holy Christian faith, of which they have left to their posterity many noble examples, and by which things they gained eternal glory and the precious evergreen crown. And the memory of these blessed doctors is a benediction in all the centuries that have been since their time and ever will be. I will be silent, then, about all these things because they are altogether too well known.

Now, we will recognize here that it is God the glorious who has exalted to such heights the most noble and most powerful kingdom of France. Who gave, to this precious pearl of holy Christendom, so worthy and excellent a name as "most Christian kingdom"? Who, I say, gave it this divine title and shining honor, if it was not because this most renowned people has guarded the purity of the holy faith without any spot since the beginning of its existence, and has always been most fervent and eagerly careful to repulse and extirpate the enemies of the salvific truth and Catholic doctrine, and to all those who left the road of true faith has been a terrible and fearsome enemy, like a very large and well-ordered army, and always has been ready to invade, crush, and repulse them?[91]

90. Dan. 6. Daniel was likewise saved by divine intervention from a grisly end when he was thrown into the lion's den by the Persian king Darius, who had conquered and was ruling Babylon, where Daniel was a royal official who refused to renounce the God of Israel.

91. The French version garbles the syntax of the long Latin period employed here; we have attempted to render the author's meaning without doing violence to the French text. In the closing lines, the French version leaves out at least one noun that would have been qualified by the adjectives *grant* and *ordonnee*; the original noun in the Latin version is *acies* and thus should be rendered "army" or "battle." See VBD, 119, note to their line 1139, including the Latin text, fol. 14a.

And can it be that the victorious Charlemagne, king of the most chivalrous French [sic], is celebrated above all other princes of the world by such singular praise and by such glorious memory, unless for his constant efforts, of great diligence and with constant labor, to enlarge and expand the limits of holy Christendom? For without resting he exalted the name of Christianity, and defended it against all enemies with great skill. Who does not know how many great triumphs and how many memorable victories he won over miscreants and enemies of the Catholic faith—mainly by the power and marvelous valor of the French [sic] knights, though he was accompanied by many other nations?

The French, therefore, have always made extraordinary efforts to support and raise up the Christian religion, and above all other nations have shown themselves to be unique champions of the Catholic faith, and from this they earned the most honorable and glorious reputation, which shines forth in all the world at all times.

And therefore, most noble, most excellent, and most brilliant princes of France, may it please you to think of these matters, may it please you to hand down to your descendants this high honor that your most noble ancestors have left to you. For God's sake, take courage and be diligent and eager to extirpate this most poisonous and detestable sect of witches, who are trying to remove from you or sully the most bright and brilliant light of your hereditary glory of purity in the holy faith. Do not be frightened by things you hear; think back, as scripture says, from generation to generation, and you will perceive that no one who hoped in God was ever kept from his good and praiseworthy desire, but always obtained glorious results from his virtuous works.[92] So do not have any fear of the lying words these execrable sinners use to frighten people.

The glory of the sinner, as scripture says, is like excrement and like an earthworm; he raises himself up quite high today, and tomorrow he is dead and there is no more news of him, for he has returned and fallen into hell, which is his own home and place due to his estate.[93] And his thoughts will perish, as scripture notes, for he finds himself deprived eternally of all the pleasures that he sought and sees that he has failed in all his plans.[94]

---

92. 1 Macc. 2:61 (VBD, 119).
93. 1 Macc. 2:62–63 (VBD, 119).

94. 1 Macc. 2:63 (VBD, 119); cf. Ps. 146:4 (KJV).

Now exert yourselves, most glorious princes, and work courageously in this most salvific task: wage this war chivalrously for the defense of the most holy faith of God, and truly this divine law will reward you for your pains with the banner of eternal glory; it will make you glorious in this world and in the other, if you strongly repulse these cruel enemies, who with all their ingenuity conspire against universal salvation. And if by just vengeance you constrain this rebellious and miscreant people to leave in peace those who wish to live devotedly in Jesus Christ, as the Apostle says,[95] you certainly will be numbered among the glorious host of the real protectors, champions, guards, and defenders of the most worthy Christian law.

[You] should abolish and erase all traces of the depraved vanities and false inventions of this accursed sect so that, by your diligence, the candle of true faith might be lit and placed on the chandelier, as scripture says, to bring light to those who are surrounded by dark shadows and who sit in the shadow of death,[96] so that they can see, thanks to this most brilliant light of the holy Catholic faith, to direct their feet on the path of salvation and eternal peace. It seems to me that according to my modest understanding and capacity, I have sufficiently persecuted and detested the abominable depravity and detestable miscreancy of the witches. And I have also declared sufficiently how their malice is execrable and dangerous. I think I have properly finished the first part of this treatise.

[PART II: HOW WITCHCRAFT IS PRACTICED]

Now the second part of this treatise begins, in which I will show in as few words as possible how the Devil can procure and work the strange and wondrous things that are said to be brought about by this damned superstition.

---

95. There is a strong echo here of 1 Tim. 2:2; Tinctor may be suggesting that it is the duty of governors to ensure that Christians may live a godly and peaceful life.

96. Ps. 107:10 (KJV) (Ps. 106:10 in the Vulgate; VBD, 119).

It is certainly necessary to be able to find the truth about these things in order to calm the disturbances that now afflict the hearts of good and loyal Christians, who, not knowing where such things come from, are overcome by such fear and wonderment that the tranquillity of their mind is much damaged and undermined. It would be a very good thing that they should learn, in all moderation and sobriety of spirit, how these things happen, such that—given the most depraved deceits of this traitorous master—they no longer wonder at such events, but rather occupy themselves solely with thinking about and admiring the lofty and most glorious works of God, and rejoice in the sweet path of his commandments. The most intelligent will learn about the truth in this way, and they will be able to teach the simple folk and direct them toward holy and salvific doctrine, and they will be able to repulse, refute, and confound those who seek to know these detestable vanities and thus hurl their precious souls into eternal damnation, and who now are—alas!—so numerous.

This teaching will thus be very useful for both teaching and practice among the good and for the overturning and confounding of the evil, and will be like a powerful and strong tower for the protection of all loyal Christians against the clever traps and harsh incursions of our mortal enemy. And so as to enter into the matter, we shall first note that this master craftsman, as he is gifted with a most acute and lively ingenuity (a magnificent gift, which, as Saint Denis [Dionysius the Areopagite] says, he preserved untouched even after he had fallen and hurtled down from heaven), and because he also has enormous power and natural force beyond nature (with which he was created, and which he did not lose when he fell), he can, by the profound ingenuity of his mind and by his preternatural power, cause and make happen most strange and monstrous things, which in the common opinion of the people are reputed to be miracles. And these things happen both truly and in reality, and at the same time are done only by clever deception and fantastical illusion, in which [the Devil] never intends to pursue any benefit for human beings, but always intends to deceive them and make their souls fall into damnation.

The theologians agree with the philosophers on this point. And this is also the foundation of the accursed and prohibited art of necromancy, and the origin of its deceptive teachings that make much use of images, mirrors, and the tricks of the demons, and recount innumerable follies about them. And there are many detestable invocations for such purposes in the books of Hermogenes and Philes, who practiced this abominable craft actively, and there are also some in the book attributed to Solomon called the *Alimandel.* And some of these invocations are found in Greece in the work of Athoc [Toz Graecus], some in Babylonia in the work of Germa [Germat], and some in Egypt, in the work of Hermete [Hermes Trismegistus].[97] But it is no easy thing to show what the power and efficacy of this art of necromancy might be, or by what means the Devil, called on silently in these invocations, is brought to accomplish the depraved desires of these magicians, and does so many wondrous works that astound the whole world. But here there are most profound and obscure difficulties, and if we wanted to address them in as much detail and as copiously as certain learned theologians and notable philosophers have done, we would need to write many long books, which might more disturb the minds of the simple folk to whom this treatise is directed than provide instruction for them.

Wanting, then, to speak of this matter in the briefest way possible, we will offer a few short points that will serve as a light that illuminates the understanding of a person so that they can see in some detail a large number of these tricks, and by which means the deceptions and malice of the Devil can most clearly be unmasked.

97. Van Balberghe and Duval report, "The source of this passage is the *Summa theologiae* of Albertus Magnus, II, 30, ii. 'Hermete' (Hermes the Egyptian or Hermes Trismegistus) is often confused with Toz Graecus (here 'Athoc'), the author of the *Book of Venus* and of the *Book of the Stones of Venus.* Germat of Babylon (here 'Germa') was an authority on the magical powers of stones. On these figures see Lynn Thorndike, *A History of Magic and Experimental Science During the First Thirteen Centuries of Our Era,* vol. 2 (New York/London, 1923), 225–228 and 719. On Hermogenes, see the legend of St. James the Greater and Hermogenes in Jacob of Voragine, *Legenda aurea* [99, *passim*]" (VBD, 119). On Alimandel, see Sefer Raziel HaMalakh, *Book of the Angel Raziel (Liber Razielis Archangeli),* a text conventionally attributed to Solomon.

The first point concerns the nature of this art of necromancy and by what means it is carried out

And although the art of necromancy[98] properly speaking contains only those divinations that are procured by speaking with apparitions of dead people, I will nonetheless use the term necromancy for all divination, including hydromancy [divination by water], aeromancy [by air], pyromancy [by fire], chiromancy [by the lines of the hand], spalimancy [by the wings of birds and the shoulders of animals], haruspicy [by the flight of birds], by augury and by all similar deceptions, which I shall not treat separately, as it would take too long and be too tedious.

And on this topic I want to affirm one thing that is most particularly to be noted, which is that all these arts are nothing but fairground tricks, lies, founded entirely on falsehood and deception, for in all these teachings, they suppose that the Devil can be forced and constrained to appear and to come to those who call him, and to carry out their desires and do their will. Whoever wants to understand these things in a catholic fashion, and as a true Christian, must consider and frequently recall the words of the most excellent doctor, Saint Augustine,[99] and then he will very easily understand the great deception of this mad and damnable art, and will clearly perceive the fanciful tales of which it is full.

Demons, says Saint Augustine, are attracted by the different sorts of stones, woods, animals, songs, and rituals, not as humans or animals hunger after food, but as spirits are called by signs. Indeed, this point is very lofty and of primary import, for it shows that whatever is done by this accursed practice comes about not by any virtue in the stones themselves or in other things mentioned, as though the Devil

98. On necromancy (from *nigromantia*, black magic), the predominant form of learned magic (widely practiced by priests) in the later Middle Ages, see Richard Kieckhefer, *Forbidden Rites: A Necromancer's Manual of the Fifteenth Century* (University Park: Pennsylvania State University Press, 1998); and, also by Kieckhefer, *Magic in the Middle Ages* (Cambridge: Cambridge University Press, 1989).

99. Augustine, *De civitate dei* 21.6 (VBD, 119).

were constrained or in any way moved and inclined by those things to manifest himself to those who invoke him and to do what they ask. And why should anyone be surprised that the Devil, who is of an incorporeal nature, cannot be forced by corporeal things? For, as Job says, there is no force on earth that is equal to his, or that can in any way be compared to him.[100]

Therefore he is not constrained by invocations as a beast is attracted by food, but because they [demons] want most of all to be treated with divine honors and are deeply envious of the goods with which human beings are endowed, and try with all their might to bring them to eternal damnation. They are quite happy to come in response to such invocations and useless rituals, for by these they assume they are being shown the reverence due to the Creator and that those who invoke them want to make a perpetual alliance with them and forge a close relationship. And by this folly, men pitiably deceive themselves, and once deceived, go without any doubt at all to lasting perdition, and if divine mercy does not benignly recall them from this deception, they will finally find themselves dwelling among the false spirits and evil hypocrites where they all will be punished unendingly.

Demons, therefore, as I just noted, show themselves to those who invoke and call them, not by constraint but of their own will, promising to help them. And yet these, his hateful servants, allow [necromancers] to continue to believe that they [demons] are forced by such conjurations to appear so that they can all the more easily tip them [necromancers] into damnation, since their thoughts are so occupied and detained by this error that they do not have time to open themselves to the salvific exercises of penitence and wholesome devotion. And indeed this accursed art is not merely useless to constrain demons, but it is also vain and unavailing to obtain those things that those who mess with this art imagine they will acquire, for the character or lines, the portraits of some kings or other, making images and mirrors, rituals involving written characters and similar follies—to which are ascribed all the power of this damned art—are in no way

---

100. Job 41:33 (Job 41:24 in the Vulgate).

able to cause real effects or to produce natural objects, for all this sort of trumpery is mathematical in character, and such things are separate, distant, and abstract, as the philosophers say, from all real and physical actions, or they are the product of clever artifice, for nature, having already attained its final and perfect form, is added to only by way of the sterile forms of human artifice, which are in all ways distant from real and true causality.[101]

The second point concerns the things that demons do in reality

There is no one with moderate experience of holy writings, and to some degree familiar with holy scripture, who can call into doubt the fact that many things happen against the accustomed order of nature by the actions of both good and wicked angels, and thus by divine command or permission.

Who has not read how the three angels appeared to Abraham in the vale of Mamre when he was sitting before his tent, and how God by the hand of these, his ministers, made fire and sulfur rain down on the five cities of Sodom and Gomorrah and the whole surrounding area?[102]

Who does not remember that by the divine command and by the service and ministry of the angels, thunder and lightning and a very thick cloud covering the entire mountain appeared, with the loud blast of the trumpet, when God wished to give Moses the law on Mount Sinai?[103]

Likewise, there are few who have not heard the story of the holy Bible telling of the host of the children of Israel fleeing the fury of the Egyptians, who were given, by divine mercy using the services of good angels, a cloud of smoke by day to preserve and cover them, and by night a column of fire to light their way and guide them;[104] and we must likewise understand the holy manna sent by God,[105] and the

---

101. The syntax of the French can be the result only of a botched attempt to translate the Latin original; see VBD, 119, note to lines 1342–46, including the Latin text and their solution to the problems posed by the French version.

102. Gen. 18–19.

103. Exod. 19:16–20; for the idea that angels were involved as intermediaries, see Gal. 3:19.

104. Exod. 13:21–22.

105. Exod. 16:4–15.

birds he made to rain down on the host of the said children [of Israel] in as much abundance as the sand of the sea.[106]

Thus also we must consider Enoch, transported to the terrestrial paradise,[107] Elijah who went up in a flaming chariot,[108] Habbakuk who was carried by horses to the kingdom of the Assyrians [Babylon],[109] the extermination of 185,000 of King Sennacherib's soldiers,[110] and innumerable other good deeds and gifts without number that holy scripture records as having been given and done for humanity.

Likewise, the holy stories speak of the punishments with which God has struck men, using the service both of the good angels and of the evil spirits, which certainly carried out the divine will with quite different intentions. And holy scripture attributed these scourges either to the justice of God, who punishes the wicked, or to his mercy, which rewards the good. And here are a few such examples: I do not believe there is anyone who doubts that a good or evil angel, by the commandment of God, suddenly sent the fire that burned and devoured the two captains and the fifty men whom each one had in his company, who had been sent in arrogance by the king of Samaria to the prophet, to inquire as to whether he would not be cured of his illness.[111] Indeed, the angels quickly carried out the divine judgment on these people who, for their grave sins, were killed by a death most cruel.

The temptation of Job is manifestly, as the truth of scripture witnesses, the result of Satan's persecution; by Satan's malice having been deprived and stripped of riches and of his descendants, Job was struck by a spotted plague and by most painful sores from the soles of his feet to the top of his head.[112]

Everyone also knows how that tempter the Devil took Our Savior and put him on the pinnacle and roof of the Temple and then transported him to a very high mountain.[113] And likewise we hear every

106. Num. 11:31–32.
107. Aquinas, *ST* III, Q. 49, Art. 5.
108. 2 Kings 2:11.
109. Perhaps a reference to Dan. 14:1–30 (Bel and the Dragon), found in the Septuagint but not in the Hebrew original.
110. 2 Kings 18–19.
111. 2 Kings 1:9–16.
112. Job 1:6–2:7.
113. Matt. 4:5–10.

day the Gospels in which are recounted the miraculous healings of the possessed, whom the kindness of Our Savior delivered from their demons, which are sometimes called in holy scripture "legion,"[114] both oppressive and destructive spirits as well as mute demons, the repulsing and expulsion of which by Jesus Christ is a clear proof and testimony of his true divinity.

And the doctrine of the holy church also teaches that at the end of the age, the holy angels will in a wink of the eye gather the dust of all the dead bodies all over the world to resurrect them and prepare them to receive everlasting life. And what can one imagine seeing that would be more miraculous, beyond the miracles of divine omnipotence, which are guaranteed by the authority of holy scripture, about which it is not allowed to entertain any doubts, than that the great multitude and, as one might say, immense forest of above-mentioned miracles are the result of the natural powers of the angels?

Now let us declare how things are done that at first glance look to be most wonderful.

THE REASONS FOR IDEAS ABOUT WHAT THE DEVIL CAN DO IN REALITY

And I will offer only one point to elucidate this, but it is of such great power and importance that it contains the entire weight of this lofty and vast topic.[115] Just as, according to Saint Denis [Dionysius the Areopagite], divine wisdom has conjoined and united the ends of primary things to the beginnings of secondary ones, it is necessary that the lowly nature and part of that which is in itself the most noble and highest thing also be touched by this high nature, and because movement from place to place is the primary and most perfect movement that exists in the physical world.

For, as Aristotle teaches, local movement does not affect or dispose toward corruption and loss of substance, which all other types and manners of movement do; for generation and corruption [decomposition] affect the substance of a thing in itself, and change, growth,

---

114. Mark 5:9.

115. As noted above, the argument that follows, which seems to have been assembled from a number of passages in Aquinas's *Summa Theologiae*, is similar to a passage in the *Recollectio* (pp. 23–24).

and diminution are preliminary dispositions to corruption and loss of substance.[116] Furthermore, local movement can be found without the other [types of movement], for in the heavens there is no movement other than local, but the other types cannot occur without local movement; it follows by necessity that if the other movements are somewhere, there is also local movement there, but the obverse is not true, for it does not follow that if a local movement is in some body, then the others must be there as well.

Then, since local movement is the first and the most perfect movement that exists in corporeal nature, corporeal nature must obey spiritual nature in this local movement. It follows by necessity that an angel can in reality do and produce all those things (and not others) that can result and occur by applying and joining locally active things to passive ones, in whichever manner. And who does not know that the Creator has given to the corporeal elements of the world a great and very ample power, which is mainly scattered everywhere in the physical world in certain secret and unknown seeds, which, variously joined and placed together, produce quite wondrous things and very strange effects, and that all these things can be done in reality by the cunning skill of the Devil?

HOW DEMONS CAN MAKE SERPENTS

By this means, the magicians of Pharaoh made real serpents out of staffs by their secret enchantments and invocations, as holy scripture witnesses,[117] and this was done by the cunning skill of the enemy who, knowing all the seeds scattered in physical objects that can be used in any way to produce such things, assembled them as it were in an

116. Van Balberghe and Duval note, "In the writings of Thomas Aquinas, *motus localis* is 'mechanical movement': 'Local movement is more perfect than the movement of growing or shrinking, and it is anterior by nature, as Aristotle proves [Aristotle, *Physica* VII 2 (260a 28)]. Therefore since all bodies in nature have in themselves a certain potential of local movement, it seems that they are all alive.' *Summa theologiae*, I, qu. 18, [art. 1], obj. 2. For an overview of the question of movements (*motus*), the position of Aristotle, of Dionysius and of Aquinas, see Dionysius the Areopagite, *La Hiérarchie céleste*, ed. G. Heil, trans. M. de Gandillac (Paris, 1970), 165–166" (VBD, 120). See also *Pseudo-Dionysius: The Complete Works*, trans. Colm Luibheid (New York: Paulist Press, 1987); Fran O'Rourke, *Pseudo-Dionysius and the Metaphysics of Aquinas* (Leiden: E. J. Brill, 1992).

117. Exod. 7:12.

instant and, joining them together in the appropriate way, produced serpents from them immediately, which nature alone can do only bit by bit and over a long time, as one sometimes finds serpents created out of rotten trees, and likewise the tree called the linden sometimes produces dragons.

HOW DEMONS CAN MAKE RAIN, WIND, THUNDER, AND SIMILAR STORMS

Likewise, demons can in reality start whirlwinds, thunder, storms, and other alterations of the air, for these things are done by the raising of vapors and the mixture of elementary qualities,[118] and for this, a certain application of seeds which the Devil knows very well can be powerful and useful.

HOW DEMONS CAN CARRY PEOPLE IN THE AIR AND MAKE THEM SEEM TO FLY

In this fashion the Devil can also easily move any body from one place to another, except to the heavens, and in very little time he can transport them great distances through the air, but celestial bodies cannot be moved by any created power or transferred from their own places.

Likewise, if God and the good angels did not block the power of the Devil, he could break the locks of doors and unlock all closures, take and carry off gold, silver, clothes, jewels, and everything they contain, likewise uproot trees or blow them down wherever he likes, raise terrible storms at sea, destroy vines, grain, and all the goods of the earth, and cause a hundred thousand other disasters to humanity.

HOW DEMONS TEMPT PEOPLE

By this art also he often tempts people greatly and horribly assaults them, and in most cases, alas, he conquers them and wins. He offers

---

118. Van Balberghe and Duval note the following: "'Elementary qualities': According to scholastic doctrine, quality is one of the nine accidents defined by Aristotle. It perfects and modifies a substance in its being and in its actions. It has four types. The elementary quali- ties are of the type of 'forces' or 'facul- ties,' that is the immediate principles of actions and of the determinations of substance. See P. Mielle, 'accident,' in the *Dictionnaire de théologie catholique*, vol. 1, first part (Paris, 1930), 302–303" (VBD, 120).

them and shows them pleasant and attractive things that he has just
created or brings from some place, making of God's creatures nets to
take people and a trap to catch them. And if he sees that he cannot
get them with this game, he attacks them by another, more cunning
art. He awakens in the person passions and physical appetites, and
subtly inquires and finds out to which sin they are most inclined; once
he knows this, he tries all means that might serve to obtain their
consent to this sin, and by one trick or the other he overturns and
slays them, unless they resist and unless they are saved from it by the
grace of God.

**The third point addresses the things the Devil does by
illusion and merely by appearance, without any reality**

Although the Devil can do many things in truth and without deception, as I have noted, nonetheless there are many others that are
beyond his power, which this lying deceiver pretends to be able to
do, and by this lying illusion leads those who serve him into damnable error.

This third point, then, will show how one can discern and know
which things are done by the Devil in reality and which are done only
by illusion and in appearance, and will also demonstrate how he does
it and how he deceives people thereby. There are four types and categories of things that are not subject to the natural power of the
angels. The first category includes the heavens, which can in no way
be changed by the elementary seeds discussed above, as they are not
susceptible to any innovation or change.

GOOD OR BAD ANGELS CANNOT AFFECT THE HEAVENS BY
MEANS OF THEIR NATURAL POWERS

Thus the eclipses of the sun and of the moon cannot be advanced or
delayed from their ordinary schedule unless by a divine miracle. Likewise, the stars of the firmament cannot be deprived of their lovely
light, although coarse clouds can hide from us the brilliance of their
rays and thus there is no change to the stars, but only in the air, and
this change can in fact be produced by the Devil, as I just noted.

ANGELS OR DEMONS CANNOT MAKE A MAN INTO AN ANIMAL
OR AN ANIMAL INTO ANOTHER ANIMAL

The second category of things that are beyond the power of angels are the natural species, which are essential parts of creation, for one species cannot ever be changed into another, just as a man cannot by some power be transformed into an animal; but everything that is reported about such deeds is nothing but deception and a false illusion of sorcery, and how this can happen will soon enough be shown.

It is, I say, impossible to transmute one species into another, because, according to the philosophers, one thing cannot be made of any other, but it is necessary that each thing made by a natural transformation be made of a specific and particular material, and that like produces like. And furthermore, since a substance cannot be created out of nothing except by an act of creation, which is a work of divine omnipotence, it is impossible in every respect that one species [be transformed into another] except only by that sacred and incomprehensible ["supermiraculous"] transubstantiation[119] that belongs only to the infinite power of the divine majesty, which our faith affirms happens in the holy sacrament of the altar, which is one of the sovereign gifts that God gives his church. But we do not intend at present to speak further on this matter; moreover, it has its own place elsewhere.

ANGELS OR DEMONS CANNOT MAKE AN OBJECT PASS
THROUGH A CLOSED DOOR

The third category of things that are not in the power of the angels are dimensional entities that cannot be together in the same place, except by a divine miracle, and that cannot interpenetrate one another or lose their proper nature and their dimensional place. Thus the Devil cannot by any means make a substantial object having mass enter or pass through a closed door. And if this seems to happen, one must say that it is either a pure illusion and phantasm without reality, or that

119. As Van Balberghe and Duval note, the syntax breaks down in the French translation, as the supplied phrase is missing. The Latin (fol. 211a in Gerson, *Opuscula*) supplies the necessary information: "impossibile est ex una substantiali specio conversionem aliam resultare nisi sola supermirabili transsubtanciatione" (see VBD, 120).

the thing one sees is an object formed of air by his cunning skill, which he resolves and makes to return to the subtlety of the air, and which he makes enter some closed space bit by bit through the fine passages that lead into it; and then he rejoins it and reassembles it again, giving it the form and appearance of a firm object, and giving it the shape and color of the object that it counterfeits. In a fairly similar manner, we see in very thick clouds the appearance of the forms of mountains, animals, or other various images. We likewise see that a rainbow projects diverse colors, which are not, however, real colors [i.e., are not actual colored objects].

ANGELS OR DEMONS CANNOT EXERCISE NATURAL
FUNCTIONS OF THE LIVING BODY

The fourth manner of things that is beyond the power of angels are the natural functions of the living body, which neither good angels nor bad can exercise in corporeal nature, for a substance that is in all regards separate from the body and that exists in immaterial purity without depending in any way on a physical object, as angels do, cannot substantially animate a body. And as the second and accidental perfection presupposes by necessity the first and essential perfection, it follows that the functions of a living body cannot take place in a body without the substance of life, and for that reason the angels cannot exercise these functions in a body that is dead. Thus, when they take a body and make it perform all the functions and actions of a body that seem to be natural functions, these are not real, but simply appear to be so.

The angels, therefore, when they speak through a body they are using, do not produce a real human voice, which is formed by breathing and by a number of organs in the human throat, such as a tube which is called by the philosophers the artery that makes the voice; but by refracting the air in diverse ways, they make numerous sounds similar to the human voice and by very clever skill know the signification of these sounds, and insinuate and address them to human beings as though they were speaking to them, which, however, as I have said, is not really human speech.

Likewise, they do not see through the eyes in bodies they possess, for they do not have any life force or capacity of sight, nor do they hear through the ears, but rather receive via their spiritual intellect all the knowledge that human beings receive through these senses. For they know and discern everything that humans see and hear; thus they answer questions and requests that people make of them and in all intercourse behave the way people are accustomed to behave with one another.

And likewise they do not really eat or drink, because eating and drinking are actions of the soul belonging to physical nature. And this truth was proclaimed by the holy angel Raphael, who came in the form of a man to accompany the young Tobias on the voyage he made to search out his wife; for after he had accomplished the errand with which God had charged him, he revealed his nature to the members of the most virtuous and well-bred house of Tobias, and said to them, "While I have been with you, it seemed to you that I ate and drank, but I take only spiritual and invisible food."[120] Although the good and bad angels employ dissimulation in such matters, they do it with quite varying intentions, because when the good ones do so, they do it for a holy purpose and for some salvific mystery. But when the bad ones do so, it is done only by perverse lies and in order to procure some great evil; and this will be more clearly stated in the fourth point.

HOW DIABOLICAL ILLUSIONS FUNCTION

And as these things are as we have said, the order that we have promised to keep now obligates us to show how these diabolical illusions are produced.

For this purpose, we need to know that the Devil tricks and deceives people into believing the illusions discussed above in two ways: the first deception comes via the external senses, such as a person's sight or hearing; and the other is procured via the interior senses, such as fantasy and imagination. And this deception of sight or hearing can be made in two ways: the first is by some change made to the organ or sensing apparatus, such as the eye, for the Devil can affect the spirits and humors of the eye in a way that changes its perception, and in

---

120. Tob. 12:19 (VBD, 120). Protestants consider the book of Tobit apocryphal, but it has canonical ("deuterocanonical") status in the Roman Catholic tradition. Eastern Orthodox Christians also consider it canonical.

this manner it can often be mistaken and deceived in its perception and can judge a thing to be of a different color or shape from that which it possesses in reality. And in this matter we are helped by the teachings of the inventors of the science of perspective, who teach that the eye can be deceived in many ways in its perception by being variously disposed or changed, as for instance if the pupil is moved a bit, one perceives a single thing as though it were two; and if it is quickly turned or shaken, it seems that one sees some light of fire, and likewise via various other movements.

The second way in which this deception is procured is via a change made in the visible thing itself, for just as the Devil can simulate any object of any color or shape he likes out of gathered air, he can also impart to an object already existing in nature the appearance of color and shape as he pleases, by gathering the air around this object and shaping it in such a way, giving it shape and color as he sees fit. In this way, a person's senses are deceived, perceiving the thing they see to be of the type and nature shown him by the image he sees, though the thing itself is in reality quite different, such as when he perceives a man to be an animal via the image of an animal that he sees. And it is no wonder if he makes such a judgment, for the philosophers say that the image of a thing among all the other common "accidents" [appearances] is that which is most expressly declared by the object's type [species].

But even if it is thus as it is said, nonetheless the exterior sense, such as that of the eye, does not err in its perception of its own material and object; for the proper object with which it occupies itself is color or shape, and this color or shape that it perceives is in fact imprinted on the air by the art of the Devil. It is not the eye that is deceived here, but it is common sense that is in this case in error and much deceived, because, as its job is to join external "accidents" to their substance, it judges this shape and color to belong to an object that does not have them, on account of the change wrought on the shape and color of the thing seen; for example, it perceives the shape of a horse or a dog to be in a person. Thus it appears to the eye that the person has been changed into a horse or dog, and yet it is not so at all. For as we have noted above, a substance cannot be transformed into another except by divine power.

In this illusion, then, neither the substance of the person nor his shape has been changed, but his image has been changed by the other image by which his is surrounded, and under this illusory image, the person is presented to the eye, from which this deception proceeds. And this truth was not unknown to Saint Benedict, as Saint Gregory says;[121] for when he had been brought a young girl who by the enchantment of a magician seems to have been changed into a mare, he knew immediately that it was a woman and not an animal and that the form of the mare was not in the maiden, but only in the eyes of those who saw her. For their eyes responded to the image that the Devil had imprinted in the air that surrounded the girl and did not receive the impression of her form.

HOW DIABOLICAL ILLUSIONS AFFECT PEOPLE'S FANTASY
AND IMAGINATION

And there is also an illusory deception of the imagination and fantasy that we see when we are ordinarily deceived while dreaming, and the manner of these dream apparitions is explained by Aristotle, who says: *How dreams are made.* "When a person is asleep and much blood descends, the movements and impressions that have remained in the faculty of perception and are kept for the intellect at that time affect his common sense, bringing him such apparitions that it seems he is moved by real things outside himself. And this can produce such a strong and vehement commotion of the spirits and humors that these apparitions can even come when one is awake, when by great disturbance and a strong impression made on the fantasy, the external senses are in all ways alienated and estranged from their proper functions, as one sees in frenetics and the possessed."[122] And these

---

121. Unclear reference. Van Balberghe and Duval report that they "were unable to find the source of this exemplum or fable via a digital search of the CETEDOC CD and a manual search of the second book ('*De vita et miraculis venerabilis Benedicti abbatis*') in the *Dialogi de vita et miraculis patrum Italicorum,* in: Gregory the Great, *Dialogues,* vol. 2, ed. A Vogüe, trans. P. Antin (Paris, 1979); F. C. Tubach, *Index*

exemplorum: A Handbook of Medieval Tales (Helsinki, 1969) contains only the story of a woman turned into a horse for poor attendance at mass" (VBD, 162).

122. Cf. Aquinas, *ST* I, Q. 111, Art. 3, which draws upon Aristotle, *De Insomniis* 3. Aristotle's *On Dreams* is one of seven short treatises that make up a collection of works by the philosopher (the *Parva Naturalia*) examining both physical and sensory phenomena.

things can be done by the Devil, and in this way he often deceives people, who while wide awake believe that they see, hear, or perform wonders, even if they see, hear, or do nothing at all.

And this manner of deception is mentioned by Saint Augustine in his book "On the spirit and the soul" [sic],[123] in which he says demons predict certain things and do quite wondrous things by which they attract and deceive many people. And hence many simple little women who have entirely given themselves over to the service of the Devil find themselves so much seduced by these diabolical illusions and fantasies that they believe that they ride in the company of Lady Herodias and Diana, goddess of the pagans, and other innumerable numbers of women. And [they believe that] the Devil shows them some pleasant and delectable things, and some horrifying and terrible things; he simultaneously shows them people they know and other people who are entirely strange and unknown to them.[124] Then the "good" master takes them through mountains and valleys, making them believe what he wants, but this takes place only in their imagination and not in reality. And nonetheless these rebellious and miscreant people believe that it is happening to their bodies in reality. And it is certain that anyone who thinks that things that exist solely in the imagination happen by real movements of the body is crazed and senseless as a beast. And up to here, these are the words of Saint Augustine.

The soul, therefore, enveloped in the aforementioned impressions, is deceived because, feeling some little interior movement, [it] believes that it is a quite large movement outside itself, as Aristotle says: it imagines that a little sound is thunder and a little light from a candle seems to be a brilliant light.[125] Thus according to the various complexions of vapors with which are mixed the images of dreams, and together these apparitions arise and differentiate themselves

---

123. Augustine, *De divinatione daemonum* (*On the Divination of Demons*) 3.4 (VBD, 121). In *On the Divination of Demons* (406), as Alan Charles Kors and Edward Peters note, Augustine "elaborated extensively on the nature and effects of demonic power." See Kors and Peters, *Witchcraft in Europe*, 43–44.

124. This is clearly drawn from the canon *Episcopi* in the tradition of Burchard of Worms.

125. Cf. Aristotle, *De divinatione per somnum* 1 (VBD, 121). Aristotle's *On Prophesying by Dreams* is another text in the *Parva Naturalia* (see above).

[*sic*].[126] Thus, that which is raised with the vapor of burnt bile, which is called melancholy, seems to be injurious, biting, sharp, trenchant, and soaked in bitter gall, and that which arises with the vapor of sweet and clear blood seems to be lovely and pleasant, and it seems that one sees or smells roses or other flowers, and likewise with the other humors.

HOW TO KNOW WHETHER THE CRIMES OF THE WITCHES HAPPEN IN REALITY OR ONLY BY WAY OF ILLUSION

Furthermore, it is important to note that the things that the Devil can do in reality by his cunning skill he normally does only by fantastical illusion. And can one know by any particular signs whether these diabolical crimes really occur or whether they happen only by imaginary illusion? If, for example, when people say they have flown or ridden with the Devil, they were absent and not seen where they reside, it is to be presumed that they really did so. But if, although it seemed to them that they had been flying, they nevertheless were seen as in everyday life, it is quite clear that it was nothing but an illusion. Likewise, when they come back from entertainments with the Devil or claim to have attended one, if they are full and have eaten well, it actually happened; but if they come back with an empty belly, they have been deceived.

And if they recognize in some other place those persons whom they have seen, as they claim, at their detestable assemblies, by that contact and acquaintance alone, it is a sign that they were there in reality; and likewise, if they bring any real thing back from these assemblies such as gold, silver, clothes, or other such similar objects that one can touch with the hand and really hold and possess, we should believe that it is not some trick they have dreamed up. And likewise in many other matters one can carefully inquire and learn

126. The Latin version of this passage reads as follows: "Et secundum variam complexionem vaporum quibus permixte sunt ymagines supermateriales et cum ceditur elevantur apparitiones hujusmodi variantur" (fol. 212b). As Van Balberghe and Duval note, "Neither the Latin nor the French version makes grammatical sense; the French is an accurate translation of this ungrammatical sentence, which is meant to explain the phenomenon previously mentioned" (VBD, 121).

about the deceits of the enemy, and by doing so, guard and preserve oneself and other good Christians from such tricks and falsehoods.

Nonetheless, I must in this matter note most particularly that one should not pursue any vain inquisitions of this sort, for by trying thus to avoid a middling danger in this human sea, one ends up plunging into another very deep gulf, this one much more dangerous. And in seeking light, one falls into deep shadows; for it is a very well known rule in sacred theology that the evil spirit comes running and joins all such vain inquisitions immediately, and that in such cases, one makes a tacit alliance with the Devil, even if one does not think of doing so intentionally. And for that reason, all good Christians must be careful to avoid all such vain inquisitions. For, as Saint Paul says, "What acquaintance should Jesus Christ have with the Devil, what communication can light have with darkness, or what partnership can there be between righteousness and iniquity?"[127]

A notice to judges. And all those who are judges of such matters should carefully weigh on the scales of reason that it does not affect the enormity of this great crime if these things are done in reality or only in appearance; for, no matter how they are done, the sentence and punishment should always be the same. Indeed, these detestable people are in no way less guilty if, following the lies of depraved spirits, they find themselves paid with tricks and full up with the wind of vanity; for the substance of the crime itself is not so much worth condemning as is the conscience of the criminal.

The doctors say: "You sin as much as you have intention of sinning, and if your eye is depraved, all your body will be made dark by it."[128] The Apostle says that everything that does not come from faith is sin,[129]

---

127. 2 Cor. 6:14–15 (VBD, 121).

128. Jean de Forda, *Super extremam partem Cantici canticorum sermones* 120.102 (VBD, 121). John of Ford (ca. 1140–1214) was a Cistercian prior and supporter of King John of England during the period (1208–13) in which the king was under papal interdict. His continuation of Bernard of Clairvaux's collection of sermons on

the Song of Songs, from which this reference is drawn, is his most important work of theology.

129. Rom. 14:23: "for whatever does not proceed from faith is sin." Van Balberghe and Duval transcribe *foy* as *soy*, which makes nonsense of the citation and does not reflect the hand in the Alberta copy of the *Invectives* manuscript, which uses a clear barred "f."

which should be understood as the theologians interpret it, namely, that anyone who does something against the judgment of his conscience places himself on the road to hell and begins to run along it straightaway.

Now, it is clear that these accursed people we are speaking of are so conscious of the diabolical things they do that they think and believe they are committing all the execrable and enormous crimes that a mouth could name or a heart could think, and that they apply all their efforts to continue in these detestable crimes, being firmly resolved to persist in this most abominable error, and without losing any of their understanding or injuring their reason, they remain in this crime. Moreover, they make an alliance with the Devil. And here lies the whole weight of this horrible crime. They ally themselves, I say, with the enemy, not as it were in passing or by some frivolous whim, but stubbornly, on purpose, and with obstinate intention, and make him their god, sacrifice to him, show him honor, and revere him as one reveres God.

Moreover, they damnably abuse the holy sacraments of the church, glory in images of the Devil, take no account of the glorious saints, and despise not only eternal bliss and the path of paradise, but in stubborn contumacy and utter obstinacy claim that there is no difference between the death of a human being and the death of an animal, and that when we die, the soul dies as the body does, and is all the same with us and the dumb beasts. This damnable error is so dangerous that once it enters a person's heart, it erases all fear and reverence of God and prevents any virtuous thought from entering.

The fourth and last point is how one can discern and know whether these aforementioned phenomena are produced by angels or by demons

As it is certain that both the good angels and the bad ones can do the things we have discussed and that they do them both in reality and in appearance, the good Christians who fear God and love his law should be most careful to know how to judge when these are works of good or of evil spirits, so that, when they know the good angels are responsible, they receive with honor and devotion their holy revelations and the good and salvific help which they, charged by God to protect his people, teach and announce, and that what they call for be done fervently and most diligently.

And in the contrary case, that one is careful to rebuff the depraved machinations of the enemy and diligent in guarding oneself against them, and to protect oneself from the clever attacks of the enemy with the shield of true and firm faith. And, as holy scripture says, God has given his friends signs and teachings by which they can protect themselves from the evil deeds of the Devil and from his misleading tricks.[130]

BY PIOUS PRAYER ONE CAN DISCERN WHETHER IT IS THE WORK OF AN ANGEL OR OF THE DEVIL

First, then, and most important for this purpose is pious and continuous prayer, for, as Saint James says, continuous holy prayer is most valuable.[131] Our Savior, certainly, as a good father and faithful Lord, will not allow us to have more temptations than we can well bear,[132] and rather he will even provide us with benefits from these temptations. And even if we stay on the holy path and in the power of the holy name of Jesus, we need help from God, for he who is truth and cannot lie has promised us thus in the Gospel: "Ask, and you shall be given."[133] And elsewhere he tells us, "All that you ask of my Father in my name he will give to you."[134]

We, then, who are on all sides surrounded by the snares of the Devil, who watches and spies on us all the time, must indeed pray for ourselves and for one another that God by his grace preserve us and defend us from these terrible dangers. And in particular we should keep vigil in prayer when we sense the disguised temptations of the enemy, who transfigures himself and takes the form of a good spirit, feigning to be an angel of light.[135] For this ravaging wolf, covered in the pelt of a simple lamb, knows very well how to attack us with deceit,

---

130. Ps. 60:4 (KJV; Ps. 59:6 in the Vulgate; VBD, 121).

131. James 5:16 (VBD, 121): "The prayer of the righteous is powerful and effective."

132. 1 Cor. 10:13.

133. Matt. 7:7.

134. John 16:23 (KJV: "the Father").

135. 2 Cor. 11:14.

and indeed the less open and more covert his assaults are, the more they are to be feared.

TO DISCERN THESE THINGS, ONE MUST CAREFULLY CONSIDER THE GOALS TO WHICH THE EFFORTS OF THE SPIRITS ARE DIRECTED

The other way one can tell whether it is a good or bad angel is by considering the goals toward which the efforts of these same spirits are directed, for the holy angel always leads us on the straight path of salvation and of lasting glory, and thus their teaching always serves to preserve and perfect the holy Catholic faith. But these damned spirits, envious of our salvation, put all their effort and apply all their skill and diligence to deceive us evilly and to falsely betray us, and always work to bring us to commit some horrible crime. And at the same time, in order to deceive us more subtly, they also make us do some things that are good and virtuous in nature, but done in the wrong circumstances and thus wrapped in vice, by which they also draw us toward damnation.

IN ORDER TO KNOW ABOUT THESE THINGS, ONE MUST CAREFULLY CONSIDER THE MEANS AND CONTEXT OF SPIRITS' ACTIONS

Furthermore, spirits can be differentiated by the means and context of what they do; for, as Saint Augustine teaches us,[136] the good angels accomplish wondrous things that they do by evident signs of public righteousness, but the evil ones do things by secret exactions, hidden agreements, and damned rituals, full of all manner of evil invention.

How the good angels employ both good and holy semblances. The good angels, therefore, when they feign to make bodies that they have taken on perform natural functions of life, are not trying to defraud anyone, but want to teach us about truth. And in order to do this more easily, they condescend to share our human frailty, and by such

---

136. Augustine, *De diversis quaes-tionibus octoginta tribus* (*On Eighty-Three Diverse Questions*) Q. 79 (VBD, 121). *On Eighty-Three Diverse Questions* was a collection of theological queries addressed on various occasions to Augustine; he wrote his replies between 388 and 395 C.E.

perceptible images as are familiar and similar to us, they allow us to know their spiritual perfection and most worthy powers; and they allow us in this painful life to savor and to taste a little bit the glorious communication that we will have with them in the lofty house of celestial glory, in order to encourage us to behave well and to yearn and burn ever more brightly with zeal for this divine habitation.

And likewise as to the prophetic visions that form in people's imagination, the good angels do not allow the prophets and holy apostles to remain in these apparitions and imaginative visions—for it would be impossible without deception and abuse—but by the figures represented to them in this way, they teach them the high and secret mysteries of the most profound judgments of God, as when he watched Jeremiah by the boiling pot and the rod, until he saw and heard, all of a sudden, that the divine righteousness, which watches over the sins of humankind, would destroy and ruin the holy city of Jerusalem and the whole kingdom of Judah.[137]

Likewise, Isaiah, seeing God in his imagination sitting upon a high and exalted throne, suddenly understood that this signified the majesty of God and his most excellent oversight of all the world, which is governed and administered by his majesty.[138]

Likewise, Ezekiel, looking at the animals and wheels that appeared to him in his imaginative vision, was instructed by holy angels that this signified the holy mystery of divine providence.[139]

Daniel also, similarly seeing a great image and statue of enormous height, knew by this and was given to understand the conduct and rule of divine providence over the government and administration of human beings.[140]

In all the things, therefore, that are done or that appear by the artful efforts of the good angels, there is no deception or vain ruse,

---

137. Jer. 1:11 (VBD, 121). Van Balberghe and Duval make a rather obscure argument that the translators attempted to render a Hebrew word game in the original, linking *shaqed* (almond tree) and *shoqed* (the watchful God) via the rather more dissimilar French words *verge* (here, for almond tree) and *veillant* (watching). VBD, 121, note to line 1913.

138. Isa. 6.

139. Ezek. 1:19 (VBD, 121): "and when the living creatures rose from the earth, the wheels rose."

140. Dan. 2. An interpretive stretch—and it was Nebuchadnezzar's dream, not Daniel's.

but all serves some high, divine mystery. And likewise there is no one of such furious malice, I believe, that he would want to tax our Lord Jesus Christ with lying because he seemed to leave the two disciples who were going to Emmaus, who constrained him to stay the night and lodge with them,[141] or when he appeared to Mary Magdalene as a gardener.[142]

On this topic, Saint Augustine says that not all that we feign is a lie.[143] It is true that he who feigns something that signifies nothing lies and tells tall tales; but when our feigning serves to signify something, it is not a lying story, but a symbol of the truth. For otherwise one would have to say that everything that has been said symbolically by wise men and holy persons and even by Jesus Christ was nothing but tall tales and lies.

The truth of such figurative speech, in fact, is not in the bark of the words and should not be taken according to the meaning that these words have on their own, but according to that which he who speaks using such symbols wants to symbolize, signify, and have understood. And as it is true that words can be feigned without being lies, one can also feign to do certain things to signify yet others—without lying.

The deceptions of the Devil are always evil and mendacious. But it is quite different with the words and actions of the Devil, for they signify lies and are nothing but trumpery and evil seduction; for even if he does some of these things in reality, they are nonetheless lies of the Devil, for he is trying by these things to defraud and deceive his subjects and knowingly to trick them.

I believe I have adequately treated this topic of witchcraft that I undertook to discuss, and if I have not said enough, I have said as much as I knew to say. I have certainly done what I could according to my loyal abilities. If any good can be found in it, I will be overjoyed and pray that God be praised and humbly thanked, as we have nothing good that does not issue and proceed from him. And if I have

---

141. Luke 24:31. He vanishes from their sight after he breaks bread and they recognize him; the author means that his disappearance was not a lying trick.

142. John 20:15.

143. Augustine, *De civitate Dei* 13.24 (VBD, 121).

failed on any point, I ask you to kindly excuse the frailty of the worker who, as Job says, has his abode in houses of earth,[144] that is to say, has a mortal body that has an end, subject to a hundred thousand imperfections and faults. I ask also that in welcoming his good will, you pray God for him, so that by the means of these pious prayers he will be able to obtain the grace of the Father of mercy, Lord and prince of all consolation, who is glorified and blessed for all ages. And so, let us put an end to this treatise.

Deo gratias.[145]

---

144. Job 4:19 (VBD, 121).   145. "Thanks be to God."

SELECTED BIBLIOGRAPHY

PRIMARY SOURCES: MANUSCRIPTS AND INCUNABULA

Brussels, Bibliothèque royale Albert I
    MS 11449–51, fols. 1r–33r (*Recollectio*—Latin)
    MS 11209 (*Invectives*—Middle French)
Edmonton, University of Alberta Library, Bruce Peel Special Collections
    MS BF 1565 T587 1465 (*Invectives*—Middle French)
Oxford, Bodleian Library
    MS Rawlinson D 410 (*Invectives*—Middle French)
Paris, Bibliothèque nationale de France
    MS lat. 3446, fols. 36r–58r (*Recollectio*—Latin)
    MS fr. 961 (*Invectives*—Middle French)
    Johannes Tinctor, *Contra sectam valdensium [Invectives]* (Latin), in
        Jean Gerson, *Opuscula* (Brussels: Fratres Vitae Communis, 1475), fols.
        202a–214c.
    Johannes Tinctor, *Invectives contre la secte de vauderie* (Bruges: Colard
        Mansion, n.d. [between 1476 and 1484]).

PRIMARY SOURCES: EDITIONS AND TRANSLATIONS

Anonymous of Arras. "Recollectio casus, status et condicionis Valdensium
    ydolatrarum." In *Quellen und Untersuchungen zur Geschichte des Hex-
    enwahns und der Hexenverfolgung im Mittelalter*, edited by Joseph
    Hansen, 149–83. Bonn: Carl Georgi, 1901. Reprint, Hildesheim: Georg
    Olms, 1963.
———. "The Waldensians, Their Sabbat, Their Evil Deeds, and How to Prose-
    cute Them, Anonymous, 1460." In *Witch Beliefs and Witch Trials in the
    Middle Ages: Documents and Readings*, edited and translated by P. G.
    Maxwell-Stuart, 79–114. London: Continuum, 2011.

du Clercq, Jacques. *Mémoires de Jacques du Clercq sur le règne de Philippe le Bon, duc de Bourgogne.* 2nd ed. Vol. 3. Edited by Frédéric de Reiffenberg. Brussels: Lacrosse, 1836.

Tinctor, Jean [Johannes]. *Invectives contre la secte de vauderie.* Edited by Émile van Balberghe and Frédéric Duval. Tournai: Archives du Chapitre Cathédral, 1999.

SECONDARY SOURCES

Audisio, Gabriel. *The Waldensian Dissent: Persecution and Survival, c. 1170–c. 1570.* Translated by Claire Davison. Cambridge: Cambridge University Press, 1999.

Bailey, Michael D. *Battling Demons: Witchcraft, Heresy, and Reform in the Later Middle Ages.* University Park: Pennsylvania State University Press, 2003.

———. "From Sorcery to Witchcraft: Clerical Conceptions of Magic in the Later Middle Ages." *Speculum* 76 (October 2001): 960–90.

Bailey, Michael D., and Edward Peters. "A Sabbat of Demonologists: Basel, 1431–1440." *Historian* 65, no. 6 (2003): 1375–95.

Balmas, Enea. "Il 'Traité de Vauderie' di Johannes Tinctor." *Protestantesimo* 34, no. 1 (1979): 1–26.

Boureau, Alain. *Satan the Heretic: The Birth of Demonology in the Medieval West.* Translated by Teresa Lavender Fagan. Chicago: University of Chicago Press, 2006.

Bousmanne, Bernard, Frédérique Johan, and Céline van Hoorebeeck, eds. *La librairie des ducs de Bourgogne: Manuscrits conservés à la Bibliothèque royale de Belgique.* Vol. 2, *Textes didactiques.* Brussels: Bibliothèque Royale de Belgique, 2003.

Broedel, Hans Peter. "Fifteenth-Century Witch Beliefs." In *The Oxford Handbook of Witchcraft in Early Modern Europe and Colonial America,* edited by Brian P. Levack, 32–49. Oxford: Oxford University Press, 2013.

Campagne, Fabián Alejandro. "Demonology at a Crossroads: The Visions of Ermine de Reims and the Image of the Devil on the Eve of the Great European Witch-Hunt." *Church History* 80 (September 2011): 467–97.

Cartellieri, Otto. *The Court of Burgundy.* Translated by Malcolm Letts. London: Kegan Paul, Trench, Trubner, 1929.

Champion, Matthew. "Scourging the Temple of God: Towards an Understanding of Nicolas Jacquier's *Flagellum haereticorum fascinariorum* (1458)." *Parergon* 28, no. 1 (2011): 1–24.

———. "Symbolic Conflict and Ritual Agency at the Vauderie d'Arras." *Cultural History* 3 (April 2014): 1–26.

Clark, Stuart. *Thinking with Demons: The Idea of Witchcraft in Early Modern Europe.* Oxford: Oxford University Press, 1999.

Cohn, Norman. *Europe's Inner Demons: The Demonization of Christians in Medieval Christendom*. Rev. ed. Chicago: University of Chicago Press, 1993.

de Blécourt, Willem. "Sabbath Stories: Towards a New History of Witches' Assemblies." In *The Oxford Handbook of Witchcraft in Early Modern Europe and Colonial America*, edited by Brian P. Levack, 84–100. Oxford: Oxford University Press, 2013.

Duval, Frédéric. "Jean Tinctor, auteur et traducteur des *Invectives contre la secte de Vauderie*." *Romania* 117, nos. 1–2 (1999): 186–217.

Duverger, Arthur. *La vauderie dans les états de Philippe le Bon: Premier grand procès de sorcellerie aux Pays-Bas*. Arras: Imprimerie de l'Avenir, J. Moullé, 1885.

Elliott, Dyan. *The Bride of Christ Goes to Hell: Metaphor and Embodiment in the Lives of Pious Women, 200–1500*. Philadelphia: University of Pennsylvania Press, 2012.

Farquhar Montpetit, Marie. "Volume of Sermons by Jean Taincture (Tinctor)." In *Canada Collects the Middle Ages/Le Moyen Âge au travers des collections canadiennes*, 80–81. Regina, Saskatchewan: Norman MacKenzie Art Gallery, University of Regina, 1986. Exhibition catalogue.

Ginzburg, Carlo. *Ecstasies: Deciphering the Witches' Sabbath*. Translated by Raymond Rosenthal. Chicago: University of Chicago Press, 2004.

Grabmann, Martin. "Der belgische Thomist Johannes Tinctoris (d. 1469) und die Entstehung des Kommentars zur Summa Theologiae des heiligen Thomas von Aquin." In Grabmann, *Mittelalterliches Geistesleben: Abhandlungen zur Geschichte der Scholastik und Mystik*, 3:411–32. Munich: Max Hueber, 1956.

Hasenohr, Geneviève. "La littérature religieuse." In *La littérature française aux XIVe et XVe siècles*, vol. 1, *Partie historique*, edited by Armin Biermann and Dagmar Tillmann-Bartylla, 266–81. Heidelberg: Winter, 1988.

Kieckhefer, Richard. *European Witch Trials: Their Foundations in Popular and Learned Culture, 1300–1500*. Berkeley: University of California Press, 1976.

———. "The First Wave of Trials for Diabolical Witchcraft." In *The Oxford Handbook of Witchcraft in Early Modern Europe and Colonial America*, edited by Brian P. Levack, 159–78. Oxford: Oxford University Press, 2013.

———. *Magic in the Middle Ages*. Cambridge: Cambridge University Press, 1989.

———. "Mythologies of Witchcraft in the Fifteenth Century." *Magic, Ritual, and Witchcraft* 1 (Summer 2006): 79–108.

Klaniczay, Gábor. "Entre visions angéliques et transes chamaniques: Le sabbat des sorcières dans le *Formicarius* de Nider." In "Le diable en procès: Démonologie et sorcellerie à la fin du Moyen Âge," edited by Martine

Ostorero and Étienne Anheim, special issue, *Médiévales* 44 (Spring 2003): 47–72.

Kors, Alan Charles, and Edward Peters, eds. *Witchcraft in Europe, 400–1700: A Documentary History.* 2nd ed. Philadelphia: University of Pennsylvania Press, 2001.

Lavéant, Katell. "Théâtre et culture dramatique d'expression française dans les villes des Pays-Bas méridionaux (XVe–XVIe siècles)." PhD diss., University of Amsterdam, 2007.

Lawrence-Mathers, Anne, and Carolina Escobar-Vargas. *Magic and Medieval Society.* London: Routledge, 2014.

Levack, Brian P. *The Witch-Hunt in Early Modern Europe.* 3rd ed. New York: Pearson Longman, 2006.

Lohr, Charles H. "Medieval Latin Aristotle Commentaries: Authors Johannes de Kanthi–Myngodus." *Traditio* 27 (1971): 251–351.

Mercier, Franck. "L'enfer du décor: La Vauderie d'Arras (1459–1491) ou l'émergence contrariée d'une nouvelle souveraineté autour des Ducs Valois de Bourgogne." PhD diss., Université de Lyon, 2001.

———. "Un trompe-l'œil maléfique: L'image du sabbat dans les manuscrits enluminés de la cour de Bourgogne (à propos du *Traité du crisme de vauderie* de Jean Taincture, vers 1460–1470)." In "Le diable en procès: Démonologie et sorcellerie à la fin du Moyen Âge," edited by Martine Ostorero and Étienne Anheim, special issue, *Médiévales* 44 (Spring 2003): 97–116.

———. *La Vauderie d'Arras: Une chasse aux sorcières à l'Automne du Moyen Âge.* Rennes: Presses Universitaires de Rennes, 2006.

Ostorero, Martine. *Le diable au sabbat: Littérature démonologique et sorcellerie (1440–1460).* Florence: SISMEL, Edizioni del Galluzzo, 2011.

———. "Un prédicateur au cachot: Guillaume Adeline et le sabbat." In "Le diable en procès: Démonologie et sorcellerie à la fin du Moyen Âge," edited by Martine Ostorero and Étienne Anheim, special issue, *Médiévales* 44 (Spring 2003): 73–96.

Ostorero, Martine, Agostino Paravicini Bagliani, and Kathrin Utz Tremp, eds. *L'imaginaire du sabbat: Edition critique des textes les plus anciens (1430 c.–1440 c.).* Cahiers lausannois d'histoire médiévale 26. Lausanne: Université de Lausanne, 1999.

Roussanov, Jessica J. "The Kings, the Dukes, and the Arrageois: State Building and Identity in Fifteenth-Century Arras." PhD diss., Northwestern University, 2009.

Russell, Jeffrey Burton. *Witchcraft in the Middle Ages.* Ithaca: Cornell University Press, 1984.

Singer, Gordon Andreas. "La Vauderie d'Arras, 1459–1491: An Episode of Witchcraft in Later Medieval France." PhD diss., University of Maryland, 1974.

Stephens, Walter. "The Sceptical Tradition." In *The Oxford Handbook of Witchcraft in Early Modern Europe and Colonial America*, edited by Brian P. Levack, 101–21. Oxford: Oxford University Press, 2013.

Tewes, Götz-Rüdinger. "Frühhumanismus in Köln: Neue Beobachtungen zu dem thomistischen Theologen Johannes Tinctoris von Tournai." In *Studien zum 15. Jahrhundert: Festschrift für Erich Meuthen*, edited by Heribert Müller and Johannes Helmrath, 2:667–95. Munich: R. Oldenbourg, 1994.

Tondeur, Arnaud. "Politique et déviances religieuses dans la seconde moitié du XVe siècle: L'exemple de la vauderie d'Arras." Master's thesis, Université d'Artois, 1997.

van Balberghe, Émile. "Les oeuvres du théologien Jean Tinctor." In *Les manuscrits médiévaux de l'abbaye de Parc: Recueil d'articles*. Documenta et Opuscula 13, 123–53. Brussels: Ferraton, 1992.

Veenstra, Jan R. "*Les fons d'aulcuns secrets de la théologie:* Jean Tinctor's Con-tre la Vauderie; Historical Facts and Literary Reflections of the *Vauderie d'Arras.*" In *Literatur-Geschichte-Literaturgeschichte: Beiträge zur mediävistischen Literaturwissenschaft*, edited by Nine Miedema and Rudolf Suntrup, 429–53. Frankfurt am Main: Peter Lang, 2003.

Zika, Charles. *The Appearance of Witchcraft: Print and Visual Culture in Sixteenth-Century Europe.* London: Routledge, 2007.

INDEX